"At Focus on the Family, we often hear from families who are watching their kids graduate from high school and transition from childhood into the adult world. It can be a challenging time for moms in particular. In *Fledge*, Brenda L. Yoder provides sensitive, biblical wisdom for moms who want to help their kids launch well."
—JIM DALY, PRESIDENT OF FOCUS ON THE FAMILY

"I found strength and hope for my motherhood journey throughout the pages of *Fledge*. . . . If you are a weary mother, you will find refreshment. If you are a weeping mother, you will find comfort. If you are still in the child, tween, or early teen stages, with a few years before your kids leave, you will find direction and practical help for the years to come."
—AMELIA RHODES, AUTHOR OF *PRAY A TO Z*, FROM FOREWORD

"How I wish this book was available before my child left the nest! Brenda L. Yoder has done a masterful job of describing decisions and strategies that will help you to transition to a good place while you learn to let go of your adult child. If you're struggling with anxiety, grief, control issues, or boundaries, read this book. The 'Building up and letting go' section in each chapter will give you questions to ponder and prayers for the journey. I highly recommend this book!"
—CAROL KENT, AUTHOR OF *HE HOLDS MY HAND*

"Clear, powerfully practical, and encouraging. A perfect blend for parents committed to navigating kids to a life of courageous faith."
—ADAM STADTMILLER, COAUTHOR OF *GIVE YOUR KIDS THE KEYS*

"There are plenty of books for mamas of little people, but almost none for moms like me: moms trying to let go. Like Brenda L. Yoder, I am experiencing 'mom grief' because things are changing. Yes, *Fledge* is for me, and I greet it with joy and relief. Finally, a voice of compassion and reason, speaking wisdom and strength into this weird but crucial season of parenting. Yoder makes me feel as if I am not alone, and for that I am grateful."
—LORILEE CRAKER, AUTHOR OF *ANNE OF GREEN GABLES, MY DAUGHTER, AND ME*

"In just a few short years, our children will be moving on to college. As parents, we really want to prepare them (and ourselves!) well. *Fledge* is exactly what our family needs: a Christ-centered perspective of the future, with the biblical tools to approach the changes well. I'll be recommending this book to all my friends in the same stage of life."
—JESSIE CLEMENCE, AUTHOR OF *I COULD USE A NAP AND A MILLION DOLLARS*

"Part devotional, part Bible study, *Fledge* by Brenda L. Yoder offers wise words to younger parents who are still in the throes of parenting. Here is a road map for launching children with grace."
—RACHEL S. GERBER, AUTHOR OF *ORDINARY MIRACLES*

"Is this your situation? 'Yikes! Just a few years ago my child was in grade school. Next year he's graduating, and there is no way I've prepared him to move out on his own!' Pick up a copy of *Fledge*. Learn how to wisely navigate the difficult passage of time between adolescence and adulthood with your child, and help prepare your child for the best that God has in store."
—JENNIE AFMAN DIMKOFF, AUTHOR OF *PASSIONATE FAITH*

"Hidden inside the celebrations of family life—the graduations, weddings, and milestones—is the pain of loss that many of us experience as our children become independent adults and no longer need us in the same way. As with all grief, unless the story of its source has purpose and meaning, it can drag us down. In *Fledge*, Brenda L. Yoder gives us that purpose and meaning and sits with us in our pain."
—CURT WEAVER, PASTOR OF CHILDREN AND YOUTH, PORTLAND (ORE.) MENNONITE CHURCH

fledge

fledge

LAUNCHING
YOUR KIDS
without LOSING
YOUR MIND

Brenda L. Yoder

HERALD
PRESS

Harrisonburg, Virginia

Herald Press
PO Box 866, Harrisonburg, Virginia 22803
www.HeraldPress.com

Library of Congress Cataloging-in-Publication Data
Names: Yoder, Brenda L., author.
Title: Fledge : launching your kids without losing your mind / Brenda L.
  Yoder.
Description: Harrisonburg : Herald Press, 2018.
Identifiers: LCCN 2017038550I ISBN 9781513802367 (pbk. : alk. paper) I ISBN
  9781513802534 (hardcover : alk. paper)
Subjects: LCSH: Parenting--Religious aspects--Christianity. I Child
  rearing--Religious aspects--Christianity.
Classification: LCC BV4529 .Y63 2018 I DDC 248.8/45--dc23 LC record avail-
able at https://lccn.loc.gov/2017038550

All Scripture quotations, unless otherwise indicated, are taken from the *Holy Bible, New International Version®, NIV®.* © 1973, 1978, 1984, 2011 by Biblica, Inc.™ Used by permission of Zondervan. All rights reserved worldwide. www.zondervan.com The "NIV" and "New International Version" are trademarks registered in the United States Patent and Trademark Office by Biblica, Inc.™

Scripture quotations marked CSB have been taken from the *Christian Standard Bible®,* © 2017 by Holman Bible Publishers. Used by permission. Christian Standard Bible® and CSB® are federally registered trademarks of Holman Bible Publishers.

Scripture quotations marked NKJV taken from the New King James Version. © 1982 by Thomas Nelson, Inc. Used by permission. All rights reserved.

Scripture quotations marked ESV are from the ESV® Bible (The Holy Bible, English Standard Version®), © 2001 by Crossway, a publishing ministry of Good News Publishers. Used by permission. All rights reserved.

FLEDGE
© 2018 by Brenda L. Yoder.
Released by Herald Press, Harrisonburg, Virginia 22803. 800-245-7894.
  All rights reserved.
Library of Congress Control Number: 2017038550
International Standard Book Number: 978-1-5138-0236-7 (paperback);
  978-1-5138-0253-4 (hardcover); 978-1-5138-0237-4 (ebook)
Printed in United States of America
Cover and interior design by Reuben Graham
Cover photo by 2nix / iStock / Thinkstock

22 21 20 19 18   10 9 8 7 6 5 4 3 2 1

To Ron, Jenna, Mark and Samantha, Drew, and Ethan: This book is the fruit of the love and joy you've brought me. I'm incredibly proud of each of you and your love for Christ.

To Mom and Dad: Thank you for teaching me independence and how to fly.

To Bob, Lois, and Catherine: Thank you for showing me how to cultivate a legacy of home.

Contents

Foreword

"*Mom*! I need help with my homework!"

I sat next to my fifth-grade son at our kitchen table and looked at his math homework: early algebra, order of operations.

I've got this, I thought to myself. So I helped him work through a couple of problems, but he questioned me at every turn. I was, in fact, wrong.

After misguiding him for three problems, I said, "Hey, buddy. How about I just sit here and watch you? I think you know what you're doing, and I'm not helping."

He looked up at me with melt-your-heart brown eyes and a crooked grin. "Good idea," he said.

After he'd finished, my seventh-grade daughter hollered from her room. "*Mom*! I need help with my homework!"

Before I plopped down next to her on her shaggy gray rug, I knew there was no helping with her math homework. Her problems might as well have been written in ancient Egyptian hieroglyphics.

"Honey, I have no idea what these problems even are," I said. "But I'm happy to sit here and listen to you work through the logic if that helps."

She nodded and talked through the problems, while I just smiled my support. She didn't need help. She just needed someone to listen.

That I can do. Math, not so much.

As my kids approach the age of leaving my nest, I hear my internal clock ticking louder each day. Five years and she's gone. Seven years and he's gone. I find myself frantic some days, listing out to my husband all the vacations we still need to take. Then I fret that I haven't instilled in my children all they need to stand their ground spiritually in this world.

I *don't* have this, I find myself thinking quite often. Social media bullying. Pornography on cell phones. Twelve-year-olds committing suicide. It all makes me want to find a remote piece of property, live off the grid entirely, and never let them enter the world. I *so* don't have this.

Yet hiding in fear is not God's design.

I found strength and hope for my motherhood journey throughout the pages of *Fledge*. Brenda L. Yoder reminds us that, yes, the world is increasingly dark, but we know the One who has overcome the world. He has equipped us with all we need to live a life of righteousness, and that includes equipping us to parent our children well, right now, in this time, in this world. Brenda shares wisdom from the pages of Scripture, from her training as a counselor, and from her own motherhood journey.

One meaning of *fledge* is to put feathers on an arrow so it can fly straight and strong. Brenda reminded me what we really are: a generation of warrior-mothers helping our young arrows be prepared for flight into the fight. If we stay closed up in our homes, hiding in fear, God will find other warriors to battle on his behalf. But why not you? Why not now? There's no one more equipped or qualified to warrior on for your children than you.

I love how Brenda teaches us that it is our responsibility to point our children to God so they can fly in the direction he has designed for them. God has a plan for them, and sometimes that plan might make us uncomfortable. But as we lean into him and deepen our personal relationship with him, we can trust that his plan for their lives is best. We can release them to God's care without fear.

If you are a weary mother, you will find refreshment in the pages that follow. If you are a weeping mother, you will find comfort. If you are still in the child, tween, or early teen stages, with a few years before your kids leave, you will find direction and practical help for the years to come. If your kids are in a variety of stages of coming and going from your home, you will find strength for these years.

Wherever you are in your motherhood journey, I invite you to stand strong. Take your rightful place as a warrior-mother. Let's learn how to help our children fledge well.

—Amelia Rhodes, author of
Pray A to Z: A Practical Guide to Pray for Your Community

Acknowledgments

It's hard to write a book that mirrors what you're living. As I put each of these chapters together, life events defined them even more. These years of letting go and transitioning are the best of times and the worst of times, and I am convinced it is the grace of the living God that sustains all of them.

To Jenna, Mark, Samantha, Drew, and Ethan. I love each of you with an unending love. You are the life and breath of this book, because each of you has seen and experienced the hand of God in our lives, personally and as a family. I am incredibly proud of who you are as individuals. I love the way you support one another. Most of all, I love the relationship each of you has with Jesus Christ.

Ron, thank you for the legacy we are creating together. Thank you for supporting every dream I have and every open door. I'm looking forward to the years of the empty nest. I love you.

To Amy Gingerich—thank you for approaching me about writing for Herald Press. Thanks to the Herald Press team for seeing the importance of this message for parents in this stage, and for giving me the privilege to publish with you! Thank you, Valerie Weaver-Zercher, for your kind, gentle approach to editing.

Thank you, Melodie Davis and LeAnn Hamby, for making this project complete.

To A.R.: thank you for all your encouragement. To my writing group and my Lake Cottage writing friends: thank you for being great cheerleaders, mentors, and friends.

Thank you to the prayer team of this project.

To my dear friends who are walking through each of these family stages with us: you know who you are. You know me both at my best and worst and still love me.

And to Mom and Dad, Catherine, Bob and Lois: thank you for the legacy you have left. My children would not be who they are without you.

Thank you to God, Jesus Christ, and the Holy Ghost. All glory, praise, and honor I give to you for my redeemed life. This is your story. Thank you for the honor to speak of you to others. I love you.

—*Brenda Lazzaro Yoder*

fledge: /flej/ *verb*

1. (of a young bird) to develop wing feathers that are large enough for flight
2. to provide (an arrow) with feathers

Introduction

Parenting is risky business. You love so deeply that when you release your children, it physically hurts. Your heart aches. It's painful, because you no longer have control.

Believe me: If you set out to write a book on releasing your kids and trusting God, he'll give you opportunities to live it out.

I hate when that happens.

Even when you're not writing a book about parenting, God allows circumstances in your children's lives that remind you that you are not in control of them or their futures.

Yet God calls us to release. He shows us what it looks like in the nature he created. When young birds' wings are large enough for flight, they *fledge* the nest. Our children are like fledglings, and we as parents are preparing them to fly.

Our call as Christians is to launch and release them to their proper places in God's plan. But doing so can make you feel vulnerable and uncertain. You don't know where God plans for him or her to land. The process requires faith: "confidence in what we hope for and assurance about what we do not see" (Hebrews 11:1).

Nothing quite prepares you for letting go or for the myriads of feelings in its wake. Whether your firstborn or your youngest is approaching high school or college graduation, you're in the season of fledging your young. Your little birds have grown their flight feathers. Maybe they've even wobbled to the edge of the nest, tried their wings, and circled back home. Now they're ready for flight.

But are *you* ready? Are you ready to release your kids into the future God has for them? Are you emotionally prepared for the revolving door of change, the "lasts," and the emptying nest? Are you ready for the years of ball games and backpacks to be over?

I'm not yet. Most of my friends and peers in this season aren't either.

This book is not for empty nesters. It's for us: the parents in the process of nudging our children out of our nest, one by one. We are the parents so busy doing life we don't think of all the changes happening until the tears, the "lasts," and the hormones take over, forcing us to embrace the fact that midlife and adult kids are upon us. It's a crazy, exhausting, and exhilarating time of life, and you may not feel equipped for it.

Fledge will help you launch your kids without losing your mind.

We can think of our children as birds fledging the nest, and we can also think of them as arrows in our quiver. God's imagery of the family is also found in Psalm 127:3-4: "Children are a heritage from the Lord, offspring a reward from him. Like arrows in the hands of a warrior are children born in one's youth." We are called to let go of the arrows God has put in our quiver. In fact, to *fledge* an arrow means to put feathers on it to prepare it to fly toward its mark. It's a good image of parenting, isn't it? Equipping your children to fly well. That's the goal of the childrearing years—to release your kids into the future God has for them. Doing so requires courage, strength, and perseverance. According to Psalm 127, *warriors* are the ones who release arrows. That seems like an accurate depiction, as we have been protecting and fighting for our kids for years. We've been warriors, in many ways.

Now it's time to let go.

Some of you reading this book have multiple children, and you're in the throes of parenting three, four, or more kids at various stages. Some of you have two children, and you feel a huge gap when your firstborn leaves. Some of you may only have one child, and the fear of loss when parenting ends in one fell swoop seems overwhelming.

No matter the size of your family, you're not alone in this stage of releasing your young. Few books have addressed the individual, personal, and family changes that happen so rapidly once kids start graduating. Your life feels as if it's slipping through your hands while you're simultaneously trying to freeze time just a little longer.

I'm writing this book because I needed something when I felt ill-equipped to handle this season's multilayered transitions. I also needed parents to walk alongside me—ones who understood how hard this stage of parenting is on many levels.

So I'm writing *Fledge* for you. And me. I hope you'll be encouraged.

Each of us have a different journey as our kids transition to adulthood, but we have many similar experiences. This book is a personal handbook, giving practical resources for situations that often arise when parenting both young adults and kids still in high school and younger. It's written from a biblical perspective that's grounded in Christ. It's honest, practical, and personal, focusing on prayer and biblical principles with real life examples. It's a memoir of sorts, designed with both you, the parent, and your family in mind. Though *Fledge* is written from a mother's perspective and addresses topics specific to a woman's midlife challenges, there are also takeaways for fathers, especially in the middle chapters on giving up control, letting kids struggle, and setting boundaries. The book is formatted particularly to equip you with personal applications and meaningful takeaways.

Each chapter includes a prayer, as well as reflective and application questions in a section called "Building up and letting go." The first part of the book is focused on parenting during this season of life; the second part centers on your personal journey as a parent. My prayer is you'll respond to every prompt, allowing the Holy Spirit to encourage, empower, convict, change, or validate something you've read. My hope is you'll take at least one thing from each topic and apply it to your life and that of your family as God is prompting you.

BEING REAL | As a licensed mental health counselor, I could give you textbook answers for this parenting season. As a former school counselor and teacher, I could offer best practices for addressing the developmental needs of kids. But that's not my style. It's also antithetical to my own needs as a parent. As a mom, I've devoured parenting books, wanting to know how to do things the *right way* for each stage. But as you and I both know by now, there's no particular right way for each child. Many parenting struggles also aren't widely talked about. In my parenting journey, I've needed practical, personal, and authentic advice from experienced parents, not just the academic how-tos.

I have needed—and still need—people to be real with me. I have needed encouragement from godly parents whose families have made it through difficult struggles with their family and faith still intact. In a culture of disconnected families, hurting teens, wounded spirits, and skeptical faith, we need hope that strong families still exist when things aren't the storybook image. This book will help you answer real, honest questions: How do you build strong roots while helping your kids spread their wings? How do you foster relationships with each child as he or she grows independent? How do you keep your own sanity with so much changing around you?

I've experienced the fledging of kids both personally and professionally and have shared personal examples and practical tips for how to survive and thrive in this transitional stage. I've tried to be authentic. Over the years of writing my blog, Life Beyond the Picket Fence, I've learned one of the greatest gifts we give one another is authenticity. It's risky to be vulnerable and real. It puts your stuff (and that of your family!) out on the table for people to judge, criticize, or leave a nasty review.

But authenticity is also a powerful tool of encouragement and human connection. So, true to my style of writing and speaking, I'll share my journey of fledging four kids, along with what I've learned as a counseling professional and high school teacher. I'll share stories about my children, husband, and others so you can learn and be encouraged. To protect the privacy of my family and others, names have been changed and circumstances have been altered slightly in some of the stories.

THIS IS US | I've been married for twenty-eight years to Ron, my high school sweetheart. He's a teacher and was also a dairy farmer for the first eighteen years of our marriage. I often say our relationship is like the one in the movie *My Big Fat Greek Wedding*. My husband grew up as one of four boys whose parents had a grain and dairy farm. It's a strong, close-knit family rooted in hard work, a strong faith, and integrity. All four sons and their wives have raised their children near the farm, and we live within a half mile of one another. We all still attend the church in which Ron's grandfather grew up, and we still farm Grandpa's land. Ron's family roots go deep, and he fledged only a quarter mile from the home in which he grew up.

I, on the other hand, am half Italian and the youngest in a family of four girls. My father is the son of Sicilian immigrants who settled in the steel city of Gary, Indiana. Though I grew up in the small rural community where Ron did, my parents lived in cities most of their lives. I was a "townie" who grew up in an iconic neighborhood in our small midwestern town. My parents raised my sisters and me with independence and expected us to fledge— to use our wings to fly high and strong wherever our adult path took us. These teachings shape much of my parenting style.

So Farm Boy married City Girl. Four children came from this union. Our firstborn, Jenna, is our only girl. She has a strong sense of nurture and justice and loves others deeply. Naturally the second mom in the house, she was the coordinator of sibling play and took care of her brothers in various ways growing up. She loves them immensely. Like most first-time parents, we fumbled through many "firsts" with her, with grave failure but also with God's grace. Jenna is currently a full-time missionary whose passion is orphan care and loving vulnerable children, which she does incredibly well.

Our second oldest, Mark, is our firstborn son. Growing up, he was the family comic but also the one each of his siblings looked up to. He is the family conflict manager, as middle children often are, knowing instinctively how to bring people together. He recently married Samantha, his high school sweetheart, who complements him in a beautiful, God-honoring way. Mark is an elementary teacher and Samantha is an incredibly talented interior designer.

Our third child, Drew, is the middle *middle* kid, as the second boy. He's loved sports since he was a toddler and is a natural athlete. Drew is quiet but is a strong, steady leader like his dad. His smile lights up a room. Drew currently plays collegiate basketball and is pursuing a career in business and sports management.

Our youngest child and third son, Ethan, is last, but not least. He's had different interests from his brothers since toddlerhood, and he has defined his own path. He is determined and hardworking, and his humor catches most people off guard. As a typical lastborn child, he has learned a lot of what not to do from watching his siblings. We're still parenting him at home during this season of fledging.

Our kids are each three years apart in school. We had twelve consecutive years of having middle schoolers, years I sometimes thought would never end. And we are constantly parenting at four distinct developmental phases. Toddlerhood to middle school. Elementary school to college. As I am writing this book, we have a high schooler, a college student, a married child and a daughter-in-law, and a missionary.

Over the years of parenting, I've been a stay-at-home mom, a high school teacher, and an elementary and middle school counselor. I'm currently a writer, speaker, life coach, and therapist. Though my professional roles have changed, my role of parent has not.

Until now. In this transitional season, things are rapidly changing, and it feels as if life is speeding by. Some days I'm a mess.

I wonder if you are too.

If so, grab this book and get a cup of coffee. Join me for this crazy season of life, when we can launch our kids without losing our minds—together.

1

You've Got Mom Grief

But his mother treasured all these things in her heart.
  And Jesus grew in wisdom and stature, and in favor with God and man.
—LUKE 2:51-52

It had been the last summer vacation with everyone home. Jenna was now settled in Mexico for her first week as a missionary. Mark was back on campus for his senior year of college. Our college freshman, Drew, was settling into his first week at the university, and Ethan's year as a high school sophomore was well underway.

I stood in my kitchen that was awkwardly quiet on the first day with everyone gone. It was just me, my cup of coffee, and a lot of tears.

I let the tears fall. I had anticipated this moment for months, facing the fact that three of my four children were fledging and the end of the childrearing years was upon me. I gave myself permission to feel, to remember, and to cry. It was full-blown *mom grief*.

Mom grief is a term I coined during the last couple of years as my world quickly changed. Grief is where I was stuck, teetering back and forth between holding on and letting go, between looking back and not wanting to look forward. Grief is your natural response to the loss of a person or something important to you. For a mom fledging her kids, there's a lot of loss.

How each of us responds to mom grief is a little different, depending on our personalities and circumstances. Yet, no matter whether we have one child or six, some feelings are the same.

Standing in the kitchen that day, I was overwhelmed by memories. In my mind I went back to the days when the kids were babies, when my love for them was so big and deep I thought I'd explode. Life was simple, but the moments were significant—reading them a story, rocking them to sleep, feeling their breath on my shoulder.

Many of us, like Jesus' mother, Mary, have pondered these moments in our hearts. I grieved because my job *rearing* these kids was almost finished. I ached for the days when the kids were young. Though they still needed me, it wasn't the same.

Other memories came. Summer days when all three boys played Wiffle ball in the front yard. Christmas vacations when Jenna directed her brothers in their own rendition of a Christmas story production. I missed tripping over Thomas the Tank Engine cars and looking for deals in the Scholastic book orders. I missed the one-on-one car rides with teens before they could drive, when the car was the place they would talk to you about school, relationships, and questions too hard to discuss face-to-face.

I longed to pray with each them at bedtime just one more time.

Then I remembered God's goodness during the hard years. The days of postpartum depression, when feelings of being overwhelmed never ended. The days my family was falling apart because of excessive busyness, conflict with teenagers, and a reactionary mom who was out of control. The days I knew I had failed, and the days that God's faithfulness answered my cries.

There in my kitchen on that late August morning, I gave in to the mom grief and wept. This crazy, exhausting, and exhilarating time of life was almost over.

THIS IS WHERE YOU ARE | "That's what I need!" a mom said when I told her the subject of this book. It's a similar response I've heard from other women: from the woman whose firstborn was about to graduate, from the mom ready for her last one to leave, and from women in various stages in between. It's a season in which emotions, changes, and experiences just can't be understood except by those who are or have been at a similar place.

It's the best of times and the worst of times all rolled into one. And some days you're just holding on.

There's no better description than fledging to describe the process parents go through to nurture, strengthen, and prepare their children before releasing them: birds developing wing feathers large enough for flight; a warrior who adds feathers to an arrow before launch. Yet with all the focus and preparation on the fledgling, no one really checks on Mama Bird and all the changes that happen when your quiver starts emptying—changes for you, your child, and your family.

We're left on the sideline, unsure of what's next.

If you're like me, you sometimes feel like you're losing your mind and your emotional composure while you're watching it all happen. I'm a strong tower one moment—like on the day of my son's wedding. Yet I fight to hold myself together the day he and his bride pack up their cars and drive away to their new home.

Without me.

The night that Mark and Samantha left for their new home after returning from their honeymoon, another mom of married boys asked me how I was doing. I was embarrassed to say what I was feeling out loud. My friend, however, just *knew*. So we sat on her porch and talked about the grief, the changes, and how releasing your kids is one of the hardest things you do.

Letting go of them is a string of lasts and big moments. The last day of elementary school, middle school, and high school. Graduations and weddings, some of them in the same year. Time moves toward these milestones at breakneck speed, and you can't stop it. You experience these events with an ache in your heart, wondering where your babies went and who you will be when the last one leaves.

You and I aren't empty nesters yet. Often, when I've lamented the "lasts," well-meaning friends in the season ahead say how great it is with kids out of the house. I've heard the infamous line: "Just wait until grandkids!" But inside, I say, Wait! I don't want to be consoled about how great life is *going* to be! This is where I'm at. I don't want anyone to take away one minute of my family life *now*.

I feel like a weird species some days, chasing my teens with the camera because every moment is a last. As my teenagers roll their eyes with every snapshot, I feel stupid and out-of-date. I also feel vulnerable, because my emotions come out of nowhere. Yet other days there's contentment, loving the moments with adultlike kids, celebrating their victories and savoring the occasions in which they treat you like a real person.

Soon after my oldest two children went to college, it seemed I was in a time warp, caught between the past and the future. I was looking back too much, longing for what was. I was also fearful of what was to come. Our life was suddenly different. I felt as if I were living someone else's life and I didn't know how to navigate it. I felt vulnerable and emotional like I did in junior high, during that awkward transition between two big phases of life.

If you've felt this way at all, *you're not alone*. You've got permission to just be *here*, no matter how it looks.

GOD'S BLUEPRINT FOR THE FAMILY | I'm what you'd call a "seasoned" mom. I'm not young, but I'm not old. My house isn't full of four kids anymore, but it's not yet empty. As I mentioned in the introduction, we currently have a child in high school, one in college, one who's married, and one who's a full-time missionary. With each child who's left for college, our family has changed and *my* life has changed. While the day-to-day chaos has lessened, there are new challenges and responsibilities, and a lot of unknowns.

Just when you think you have something figured out, circumstances change.

Though I'm a counselor, I've learned nothing quite prepares you for *your* journey of releasing your kids—each one—whether it's one, two, four, or more.

Nothing, that is, except for Christ and his Word.

Nestled in the Bible is God's blueprint for the family. Throughout this book, we'll dive into Psalm 127 while also looking at other Scripture specific to the fledging experience. We'll talk about the growing pains of your children, your family, and you. In Psalm 127, God uses arrows as the metaphor for the releasing of children. Our children are in God's hands like a bow and arrow in the hands of an archer. Their Creator aims their arrows at something we can't see. Our responsibility is to put the feathers on that arrow, let go of the string, and let it fly.

But letting go, and the preparation to do so, isn't easy. Modern media would have you believe family life is made up of iconic moments and simple 1-2-3 parenting. Scripture says something different. Psalm 127 contains powerful words regarding the family: Builders. Guards. Toiling. Warrior. Love. Heritage. Reward. Blessed.

These words depict both positive and negative feelings and processes. The descriptions are intense, strong, and difficult. They are also beautiful, safe, and satisfying.

Doesn't that describe the parenting journey? The season of raising and releasing has both highs and lows, blessings and hardships, ease and adversity, love and grief.

TYPES OF GRIEF | Parent grief includes both tangible and intangible losses. You miss your child or children who go to college, move out, or get married. You miss their laughter, activities, unique personalities, and what they bring to the family. There's a lingering sadness you don't expect. A box of elementary school papers might make you cry. You share less on social media because your Bigs don't want their stuff out there, but you linger at photos of other, younger families, wondering where the time has gone.

Such sadness is just one aspect of grief as your family changes. Another kind of grief is missing the family you've known up to this point. That family has been your "normal" for almost two decades. Kids' activities and day-to-day happenings bring a comfortable, familiar routine. I miss the preadolescent and elementary years, though they were hectic. I miss the wonder of childhood and things that only happen with little ones.

And then there are the physical changes and losses that happen during midlife. If you're a mom who loved pregnancy, babies, and toddlers, you may grieve the physical loss of childbearing or what it represents, regardless of whether you want more children. A fertile womb represents youth and life: the end of childbearing represents a permanent ending to something very personal. The irony, however, is that a woman's body experiences similar hormones and emotions in both pregnancy and midlife. A fellow fledging mom said it well: we shed tears when we carry a baby and give birth, and we have similar emotions when it's time to release. Other experiences in a mother's life are outside her body; a child leaving is intricately tied to a mother's body, soul, and spirit.

There's grief of another kind—the grief of regret. As a particular child walks out the door, you may regret the mistakes you made with them, some of which may be significant. We each do the best parenting we can, given what we know at the time. We learn from those mistakes and are often better parents with our younger kids. Fortunately, God is the Lord of grace. He is the redeemer of the years the locusts have eaten, as described in Joel 2:25. This verse has become a significant promise to me as a parent who knows the grief of regret. It's also a promise I have seen God fulfill in my life and others.

We may also feel regret for our kids whose childhood experiences have been painful because of their own choices, the behavior of others, developmental challenges, or circumstances that prevented natural child development. You regret your children didn't experience the happy, carefree childhood you wanted for them or that they didn't experience success according to the world's standards. Though we hate to admit it, society's norms influence our parenting hopes and dreams.

Regret is a pain that's etched on your heart. It's something you often don't talk about. We'll talk more about these hurts later in the book. For now, just know you're in good company.

Then there's the grief of disappointment in the young adults you've raised. Some may not be flying very well or might be living a life you never thought a child of yours would live. Or perhaps you're disappointed when your young adult children don't call, come around, or even acknowledge your birthday or Mother's Day. Disappointment grief reminds you of all the things you've done for your kids and reinforces the hurt of disregard and disrespect.

Yet there's another kind of grief for those who have lost communication or relationships with their children due to divorce or addiction or estrangement. These losses, too, are rarely talked about in the Christian community, yet they're real. The hurt is deep: a gaping wound you bury so no one sees, but its dull, sharp pain reminds you of your suffering and your child's absence from your life.

And then there's, perhaps, the deepest grief a parent can experience: the loss of a child by death, whether by miscarriage, stillbirth, abortion, or a childhood tragedy. As other kids reach milestones, the reminder of what your child would be doing or who they would be brings fresh promptings of the grief and emptiness that nothing can replace. The death of a child is a deep loss only those with similar experiences can fully understand.

For women, all this grief is compounded by hormones, emotions, and loss of identity as *Mom*. There's uncertainty and insecurity as your role and relationships with your kids change. Until you're more accustomed to parenting adult children, you're in uncharted territory. It can feel scary and often lonely, because your spouse can't fully identify with your experience of motherhood. Kids are embedded in our lives differently than they are in their fathers' lives. A father's identity and role are different from ours, and they may not have the same emotional attachment to the memories of our children's childhoods. Neither is more or less significant than the other; it's just that mothers and fathers may experience this season differently.

My husband, Ron, and I have experienced this several times. The day we dropped Jenna, our firstborn, off at college, his tears fell for an hour as we began the long, quiet drive home.

My cheeks were dry after a few minutes. "I've been crying all year and you thought I was crazy!" I told him. He had often gently teased me when I cried at milestones throughout her senior year. I had felt the loss over several months, while it suddenly crept up on him on drop-off day. The same has been true as we've experienced our first wedding and an emptier house. Many times I simply have to tell him, "I really miss our kids."

It can feel lonely when your spouse doesn't share your emotional responses to milestone moments, of which there are plenty during this season. It is lonely, too, when you're parenting alone due to death, divorce, a disengaged spouse, or a father who has been absent from your child's life.

That's when we need other women who are walking through similar mom grief, like the ones who reached out to me on Mark's wedding day. Two texts came from mothers of adult boys who understood, before I did, the awkward feelings I would have realizing my role in my son's life was forever changed. Their comforting words helped me in moments when I felt those familiar feelings of vulnerability and uncertainty.

Those friends extended grace when I needed it, letting me know my feelings were normal. I hope you, similarly, are encouraged by the different topics in this book. Some experiences might be new to you, some might be where you are at right now, and some information might prepare you for a future you don't yet know.

And some of you might check off the "been there, done that" box. Either way, we are *here*, together.

GRIEF AND GRACE | We moms need to help each other accept this season with grace. Grace can mean a couple of things: the undeserved favor of God, and simple elegance of movement. I like those descriptions because most days I desperately need them both.

As you and I move from full house to empty nest, we need God's unmerited favor because many of us may feel exhausted or worn out. We've given everything we have to our kids: our time, energy, worry, and love. We've made meals, wiped bottoms, dried tears, and have done a million things no one has ever noticed.

We haven't done it for the applause. We've done it because we love our kids with an affection so deep we can't explain it. It's the love that makes sense every day of life until it separates from you, and you realize love has a name—the name of each of your children. They may never know that while they separate from you and live their own lives, they're still part of you.

This ripping away hurts. And undeserved favor is just what we need.

I also need the other kind of grace—to move through this season with elegance. Most days, though, I don't feel elegant as a woman who's losing my mind and the life I've known for twenty-five years. If I'm falling apart, at least let me look like Katharine Hepburn while doing so.

I need grace, and a lot of it. I also just need to know I'm normal, not alone, and I won't feel this way forever.

Mom *grace* is being honest with ourselves and each other about loss, midlife, and releasing kids in a way that honors yourself, your family, and where you are. It allows you to hold your head high as you walk into a new normal of life without kids.

These fledging days are beautiful: some are filled with deep loss, and others great joy.

This is where we are. You have permission to feel it all. And in every moment, just give yourself grace.

BUILDING UP
and letting go

Father, thank you for being with me in my mom grief. Thank you for letting me know I'm not alone in the changes that seem so rapid and out of my control. Help me as I walk through this season to rest in the assurance of your presence. Amen.

1. How would you describe your mom grief?

2. What are the things you miss the most as your kids grow and leave?

3. What is one truth you can encourage yourself with when you or your emotions feel out of control?

2

Let God Build
Your Family

Unless the Lord builds the house, the builders labor in vain. Unless the Lord watches over the city, the guards stand watch in vain. In vain you rise early and stay up late, toiling for food to eat—for he grants sleep to those he loves. Children are a heritage from the Lord, offspring a reward from him. Like arrows in the hands of a warrior are children born in one's youth. Blessed is the man whose quiver is full of them. They will not be put to shame when they contend with their opponents in court.
—PSALM 127

When our children were young, a friend gave me a wall hanging with the first verse of Psalm 127 written on it: "Unless the Lord builds the house, the builders labor in vain." As a young mom, I longed to raise a family that would love and honor God. So I read the parenting books. Ron and I took a Christian parenting class that we, in turn, taught at our church.

I followed the "successful parenting" formula. I hoped when my kids were older, they would rise up and call me blessed (pronounced BLES-sed), just like it says in Proverbs 31.

Twenty years later, that wall hanging is stashed in our basement—along with Hot Wheels, Barbies, Golden Books, and other
things from the early parenting years. Today they are lost remnants
from the years of hopes and dreams.

Because other things took over our house. Things like sports
schedules, carpooling, work responsibilities, moody teens, and
conflict. I forgot about that Bible verse until our life was a mess.
For some of you, the childrearing years challenge everything you
know about life, faith, and yourself. Those early hopes and dreams
get stuffed away due to busyness, immediate demands, and unexpected trials.

Why are *warriors* the image God uses in Psalm 127? Because
most parents have some type of battle scar from the years of raising kids and releasing young adults—a rebellious child, mental
health issues, a struggling or broken marriage. These are just a
few of many things you never anticipated as a Christian trying to
parent well.

I appreciate Psalm 127 differently since I've been in the battle.
The verses provide promises, truth, and a pattern for parenting
over a *lifetime*. Like a warrior releasing arrows, I've learned it
takes strength to parent in hard places. It requires perseverance
to fight for your child, teen, or young adult's emotional, mental,
spiritual, and physical well-being. You need to be girded by the
Lord himself to help each child transition to adulthood with their
health and safety intact.

While doing this, you're also letting them go.

Sounds exhausting? Many days it is. We can't do it without
surrendering ourselves and our kids to Jesus Christ.

Unless the *Lord* builds the house, our labor is in vain.

THE MESS I MADE | Currently, my kids are at good places. But
it hasn't always been that way, and I don't assume it will be all the
time. Christians are not immune from adversity, and real life isn't
a fairytale. Our parenting efforts are in vain, however, when we
do it in our own strength without letting God be the foundation
and Master Builder. We can also damage our family in the process.

I know. Here's how I made a mess of our home.

For several years, our life was crazy. We were a dual-career family with kids at different stages, from high school to elementary. The school calendar and kids' activities overtook our life outside of work. Ron and I were both high school teachers, and he was also managing the family dairy farm. As a mom and a teacher, I was stretched between balancing lesson plans, grading papers, and chasing my own kids around. Teaching surly high schoolers left me with little tolerance or emotional energy for my own teens, preteens, and Littles. After getting up at 5 a. m. to get myself, my lesson plans, and the kids to school on time, then spending eight hours with moody, irritable teens at school, I'd walk in the door at 5:30 p.m. just ready to drop. Yet, I still had 150 or more papers to grade. But now *my* kids needed something from me. The minute I got home, a chorus started of "Mom, I need help with my homework. Do we have any snacks? Where's my volleyball uniform? Mom, mom, mom . . ." I wanted to scream.

I did scream. I usually had zero tolerance for any rude or snarky attitudes from my own teens. "Mom, why do I have to do this?" or something similar would send me into an irritable or reactionary response, like "Because I said so, and I'm the mom! That's all the reason you need!" A teen's response of "you don't understand" would evoke a power struggle for the one-up. I had mom rights and wasn't going to surrender them. This cycle created a climate of conflict and turmoil which hung over our home, like the charge in the air just before a storm strikes.

Add to these dynamics my own insecurities, idealistic expectations, childhood hurts, and emotions. There's a saying which says "If Mama ain't happy, then no one's happy." My stress and irritability affected everyone. When I lashed out at one of the older kids, the conflict filtered down the family food chain. Yelling and arguing were normal.

By my late thirties, I was a parenting fail. My marriage was also strained. I'd lash out and fight with Ron, in addition to the kids. Our communication patterns were a byproduct of our different families of origin. I was verbal, direct, and filled with emotion. He, in turn, avoided direct conflict. I yelled, and he withdrew.

In those years, I often crawled into bed feeling as if my head were pinned against the wall and there was no way out. I didn't like who I had become and would ask God for forgiveness, intending to do better the next day. I was exhausted, empty, and emotionally depleted. I hoped the next stage of parenting would bring respite.

Yet, I realized the next stage would be when Jenna was in college, and Mark soon after that. If I waited until they left for college for a less stressful life, the memories my kids would have of their childhood would be of an angry, contentious mom.

It was not the legacy I wanted to leave. My home-building efforts were in vain. I was hurting my family by not yielding my rights and reactions to God.

I had one chance to parent and only three more years with all the kids at home. I had to address the unhealthy areas of my life *now*. I couldn't wait for fewer kids in the home to make me less irritable. I couldn't blame others for how I behaved. I could only change the areas of life over which I had control.

Excessive busyness was one element of stress. During the fall of Jenna's sophomore year in high school, I resigned from extra responsibilities at school and church to reduce stress. However, that same fall my classroom attendance soared to 180 students. I requested additional staff for our oversized classrooms, but it was not in the school's budget. I couldn't keep up with my family's needs in addition to the needs of 180 students. I needed respite *now*, not next year or the next year. I looked into a sabbatical, but I didn't meet the requirements. I finally considered other career options outside of education, where grading and lessons plans wouldn't follow me home.

The best solution for our mess wasn't waiting for next year or the next season of life to fix things. It was taking care of problems in the here and now. At forty years of age, I took a risk and switched professions so I could have options for a more flexible schedule and less stress at home. I packed up my classroom, started graduate school, and left the career I loved.

It was the hardest yet best decision of my life. I handed the blue-prints of our home over to Christ. He has been faithful ever since.

THE ROLLERCOASTER RIDE | I wonder if you also live for the next week or month or year, looking to the next phase when you think things will slow down or parenting kids will get easier. The school calendar dictates your life, activities, and priorities. Then next year is suddenly your child's senior year, and you can't believe he is that old. He graduates, and a whole new dynamic takes over your family. You get whiplash trying to figure out what's going on as your child pushes the boundaries, disrespects you, and yet tells you he loves you every time he calls.

Even if you don't have the stress in your life like we did, the fledging season has its own unpredictability. Navigating experiences with each kid brings its own angst and frustration.

When we dropped Jenna off at college, it was hard for all of us, including her younger brothers. Leaving your firstborn and only daughter at a university eleven hours away had a lot of "big moment" emotions. When our second oldest, Mark, graduated, I anticipated nothing different. He was my first son to leave home, and it seemed everything that summer brought tears.

Except, surprisingly, the moment of the Great Goodbye.

Ron and I took the younger boys with us to move Mark to college, as we had when Jenna moved. There was a convocation for families, and then parents were expected to say goodbye and leave campus. I was hovering around, trying to get that last family photo of Mark and his brothers to forever cement this important day in our lives.

One simple picture was all I asked for. One disrespectful answer is what he gave me. He refused to let me take one more photo of him and his siblings before we left. His brothers took his cue and rolled their eyes too.

That's when I remembered why you drop nineteen-year-olds off at college. Because it's time for independence and separation.

Goodbyes are easy when your kid ticks you off. There were no tears for that kid that day. Ron even asked me, "No tears?"

"No," I said. "I'm ready for him to go."

That's just one example of the emotional roller coaster of different kids in and out of the home. Releasing young adults while still having kids in the nest stretches you. In some families, these changes happen quickly if your kids are close in age. For others, the span is longer.

There are thirteen years between the time Jenna entered high school and when Ethan, our youngest, will go to college. That's thirteen years of moodiness, peer pressure, and family changes. Some days I literally don't know who's coming or who's going. I fill two shopping carts full of groceries, only to be told three days later there's no food in the house.

Some days I feel like a rock star. Other days I think I'm losing my mind. This season is crazy. Your house is full one moment and empty the next. And you worry whether you got it right or whether you're doing it all wrong.

Are you stressed with all the changes happening in your family? The good news is that no matter how much you or your family changes, God doesn't (Malachi 3:6). And neither do his principles for families.

THE FOUNDATION | Nestled in Psalm 127 is God's blueprint for the family. The principles are relevant to your family no matter what generation you're parenting in. It's why they are the cornerstone for this book (we'll talk in depth about this psalm in chapter 4).

I didn't really know what it meant for the Lord to build my house or to watch over my family until I had done it all wrong. I thought it was *my* job to raise my children up in God's ways. It is, in a way. But our efforts are in vain when we do it on our own. I learned the hard way. *God* has to build both the house and foundation so they are strong when it's time to let go.

"Like arrows in the hands of a warrior are children born in one's youth," the psalmist writes. As a younger parent, I didn't know releasing my kids would require warrior-like stamina and determination. I understand it now, though, because I've waged spiritual battles for my kids through peer pressure, insecurities, discouragement, and some really dark places.

Do you need God's strength to build a family foundation that will stand the test of time? Do you need him to build you up so you can release each child with confidence and strength, no matter what storms rage around you?

Fledging kids is not for wimps. It's for warriors. Parents battle both on earth and in the heavenly realms for the hearts and souls of their children. Just when you think you have something figured out as a parent of teens, it's irrelevant because our culture is changing so quickly. A cultural standard that may have been true for an older child is no longer relevant for the younger one. I've worked with teens for more than twenty-five years as a youth worker, teacher, and counselor; I've seen and heard just about everything. Amid change, challenges, and uncertainty, there's one thing I do know for certain: God's unchanging nature and God's Word are the only things that stand the test of time.

Parenting theories come and go. Current trends can sideswipe your core principles and values. Pressure from peers, both yours and your kids, will tempt you to doubt that God or Scripture has anything relevant to say about what your kids need. But trends are fleeting. Human theories are flawed, and research has margins of error.

A foundation built on Christ doesn't change, isn't flawed, and has no errors. It's the best practice there is. Let him, not you, build your house so it can withstand the strong winds and storms that will hit your family.

You are a warrior: your strength comes from Jesus Christ, the cornerstone and foundation on which your family rests.

BUILDING UP
and letting go

Father, thank you for being the sure foundation on which my family stands. Help me to release every area of our family life to you, the Master Builder. Thank you for walking with us through these changes. Amen.

1. What's the most difficult aspect of this stage for you right now?

2. What areas do you need to release to the Lord so that he is the one building your family, not you?

3. What's one principle you can apply to your life today?

3

Cast the Vision

Where there is no vision, the people perish.
—PROVERBS 29:18 KJV

I walked into Mrs. Martin's kindergarten classroom with Jenna. She wore a rust-colored shirt and a plaid skirt with a felt name tag pinned to her chest. She was excited for her first day of school. I was eight months pregnant, and my toddler was tagging alongside. Mrs. Martin looked up at me and smiled, knowing I was dropping off my firstborn for her first day of school.

I turned the corner after saying goodbye, headed toward the car, and burst into tears. I had so many emotions. Fear. Sadness. Biggest-moments-of-life feelings.

And heartache.

The ache of your child growing up, reaching milestones, and moving on to the next stage. Ache of a love so deep that it hurts, because it's outside of yourself and you can't grab hold of it.

I've felt that feeling several times since Jenna went to kindergarten. The day Ethan turned four, when I realized we were done with the toddler years. The day I realized Mark's girlfriend, Samantha, needed to take priority in his heart over me. The day Jenna boarded a plane for Guatemala to fulfill her dream for long-term mission work, knowing she'd never be the same when she came home. That first meal after Drew left for college when there were only three of us at the dinner table, along with a loud, awkward emptiness.

These surreal moments tell you life doesn't stand still and childhood has an abrupt ending. How do you stay focused on the end goal of parenting while also letting go at the same time?

THE GOAL OF LETTING GO | As the leaders of your family, you and your spouse must keep the vision of releasing your children within your sights. Otherwise, you'll be caught up by the daily demands of homework, sporting events, and another school year. Busyness and other obstacles can distract you from successfully nudging your kids from the nest. Some days you really don't even *want* to push them toward independence. Instead, you want to freeze time as it quickly passes by. But time doesn't stop, no matter how much you want it to.

Proverbs 29:18 implies that without a clear vision from a leader, those in their care perish. As parents, you and I must have a clear vision of releasing our kids because doing so isn't our natural response. You kind of take possession over your children the moment they come home from the hospital or when those adoption papers are signed. Have you ever thought or said, "They're *mine*"? Your children are dependent on you from the start, and you respond by taking care of their needs. Day by day they grow, reaching milestones of independence and autonomy. Walking and talking. Needing you less and less. Developing likes and dislikes and not wanting to obey when you know best.

Independence, autonomy, and letting go: it's the parent-child struggle that continues for a lifetime. As a young parent, you don't envision tension and struggle as part of the package. Instead, you dream of influencing your kids, loving them, and receiving their love in return. Parent dreams are happy dreams—being a good mom or dad, having a great home, and raising kids who make you proud. But letting them go? That picture isn't first on your radar.

Yet those idealistic dreams were quickly dampened when your newborn cried all night. When the first child said "I hate you" and shut the door in your face, you met reality. During these moments, you're reminded that raising kids is not for the faint of heart.

A magnet on my refrigerator reads, "To become a mother is not hard—to be a mother is." I bought it when being a mom of four kids wasn't fun. When your kids talk back and shut you out. When those once-cute kids hurt you and loving them is hard.

Toddlers become teenagers, seemingly overnight. Their love, energy, stubbornness, and mess are ironically the same. So is their quest for independence. You bring them home from the hospital, yet they are naturally positioned to walk out the door . . . like arrows in the hands of a warrior.

And your natural intention is to hold them close.

RUN WITH PERSEVERANCE | Releasing our kids would be easier if we just had to feed, clothe, and shelter them for eighteen or twenty years. But they require much more from us as parents. Our job isn't just to aimlessly let those arrows go. We are to cast Christ's vision for adulthood. We're to raise adults whose hearts are positioned toward God, reflecting God's character according to their unique, individual makeup. We do all of this for God's glory, not our own.

Our youngest, Ethan, is a long-distance runner. No matter how many races he runs, he has to strategically prepare because each course has unique challenges. He must have a particular strategy to run each course well.

The same is true for your family. No matter how many kids you're raising, they all are unique. Releasing each of them requires intentional strategy and energy all the way to the end. For one child, the experience may be relatively carefree. For another, you may go against incredible odds just to get her to her high school graduation.

"Parenting is exhausting," one mom told me. Her oldest was a middle schooler, and she had two kids behind him. I smiled, having had middle schoolers for over a decade. Raising middle schoolers is God's way of paying us back for the grief we caused our parents.

Staying focused on God's intrinsic goals in addition to worldly expectations is also challenging. God's ways are not of the world. Holding kids accountable and teaching and training them in Christ-honoring ways is hard. Without keeping God's vision in the forefront, it's easy to be completely immersed in the here and now of parenting for pride, performance, and comfort.

As a parent, you are a protector, provider, and nurturer of your child's emotional, spiritual, vocational, and relational development. This calling requires perseverance. Add in a child with a strong will, challenging temperament, or one with a particular physical, mental, or behavioral need and parenting becomes even more challenging.

Fortunately, God doesn't leave us to do it alone.

Hebrews 12 talks about running with perseverance the race marked out before you. In the parenting race, we need to focus on letting go while also noting each developmental milestone for our children along the way. If you get sidetracked by the demands of life, your child will literally grow up before you know it and you'll suddenly wonder what you were doing along the way.

How do you stay focused during these years? God's Word says, "Let us throw off everything that hinders and the sin that so easily entangles. And let us run with perseverance the race marked out for us, fixing our eyes on Jesus, the author and perfecter of faith" (Hebrews 12:1-2).

Daily demands will distract and tempt you to focus on your child's outward appearance and successes rather than Christ's vision. God would have you invest more deeply into your child's character and relationship with him. "People look at the outward appearance, but the Lord looks at the heart" (1 Samuel 16:7). While I'd love for my kids to be financially successful after college, it's more important they have kind and compassionate hearts that are tender toward God. If we're not intentional and focused on God-centered characteristics, it's easy to get caught up in success-driven priorities during the busy years of parenting.

**PERFORMANCE PARENTING VERSUS RELATIONSHIP PAR-
ENTING |** Success based on performance is a worldly trap we
parents get caught up in. From the time your kids are little, they
learn to perform. They receive praise when doing something right
and earn rewards for behaving a certain way. They are criticized
for not meeting expectations and are told they can do better even
when they succeed. Even though parents don't intend to, parents
send children an early message that their worth is based on what
they do, not who they are.

This performance mentality increases through school, activities, and sports teams, where letter grades, rewards, and goals send
them performance-based messages. Incentives have practical value,
but kids can begin to view their identity and worth as dependent
on external affirmations like rewards. This can lead to legalism
and works-based identity.

This approach is different from God's. God is a God of relationship, not legalism or performance. He created us to have a
relationship with him through his Son, Jesus Christ.

The opposite of performance parenting is relationship parenting. Your child wants a relationship with you more than he wants
praise, no matter the age. Without an authentic relationship, he
craves your praise because it's the only affirmation he receives
from you. This doesn't reflect the heart of the heavenly Father.
God loves *you*. Because God wants a relationship with you, he
provided payment for your sin through the death and the resurrection of his Son, Jesus Christ. When you have a personal relationship with God, you know he loves you regardless of whether
you succeed or fail. That's the full grace of Christ: you can't do
anything to make him love you more, and there's nothing you can
do to diminish his love.

When you experience Jesus' unconditional love, you do what
pleases him out of respect, love, and devotion, not out of fear or
performance. Kids respond to us in similar ways.

Some parents fear their children will grow up spoiled and
unruly if they love them with unconditional regard. Love *does*
need to be partnered with boundaries and accountability. Rules

with a relationship creates security, whereas rules without a relationship lead to rebellion. Teens embrace rebellion naturally when separating from parents during adolescence. But if you have an authentic relationship with your child, it's more likely she will understand that the rules you set are for her protection.

This is similar to God's relationship with us.

When your adult child separates from you and develops her own thoughts, values, and identity, your relationship is what remains. If that relationship is based on performance, she will continue to strive to please you in order to receive your affirmation, value, and love. She will also feel rejected if you only focus on her lifestyle or beliefs that are different from yours or how you raised her. These unhealthy perspectives give your teen or young adult a faulty picture of a performance-based God.

CASTING THE VISION FOR EACH CHILD | A comment made by a young adult grieved me. Alanna said most of the young adults she was hanging out with were either agnostics or atheists—and most of them had been raised in the church. Young adults are leaving the church in large numbers. Something in our faith community has gone awry. However, I'm a firm believer it's through relationships that prodigal children will return.

As Christians, our most important parenting goal should be the same as God's: that *all* have a relationship with him through his Son, Jesus Christ (John 3:16). We are entrusted with our children to *draw* them to Christ, not to *make* them choose him. We can't make our kids perform themselves into a relationship with Jesus. You also can't make them be Christians just because you are. They have to choose him, as you did. Attending youth group, memorizing verses, and performing in the worship band: things like this can become a checklist of legalistic Christianity if there aren't authentic relationships in both the church and family. We are given the privilege to cultivate hearts in our children that will be open and drawn to God. We do that by reflecting God in our own lives, by the relationship we have with our children, and by honoring, loving, and respecting Christ in our homes.

Loving your kids through authentic relationships is the greatest way to open their hearts to Christ. They don't have eighteen years to make a decision about God—they have a lifetime.

As you work through the questions in the last section of this chapter, keep your relationship with your children your main objective. It will be the bridge through changes and adversity, and will keep them headed in the path God has for them.

Consider the vision you want to cast for each of your children, no matter their age, in the following section. Keep these goals in sight while also focusing on Jesus's desire for a personal relationship with them.

The journey to release is right in front of you. Keep your vision clear for the health and heritage of your family.

BUILDING UP
and letting go

Father, thank you for loving my children more than I do. Thank you for having a lifetime path for them that you, not I, are in charge of. Equip me to focus on my relationship with them through drawing closer to you. Amen.

1. Consider each of your children at their current stage of development (even those who are young adults). What are your intrinsic hopes in each developmental domain?

   • Emotional:

   • Behavioral:

   • Social/community:

   • Relational:

   • Spiritual:

2. The above hopes become guiding principles for your parenting in the final stretch of fledging. However, these hopes should not drive performance parenting. Do you struggle between performance parenting and relationship parenting? What challenges you?

3. How can you focus more on relationship parenting?

4. What area is God speaking to you about personally after reading this chapter?

4

Define Your Strategy

Children are a heritage from the Lord, offspring a reward from him.
  *Like arrows in the hands of a warrior are children born in
one's youth.*
—PSALM 127:3-4

"He made it. I didn't think he would," the mom told me at her
son's graduation party. She was in tears the year before at parent-
teacher conferences. She didn't know if her son would make it aca-
demically, mentally, or emotionally. He was once a sweet kid but
had become defiant and oppositional. He was struggling to pass
his classes and stay out of trouble. The parents couldn't believe
these problems were happening to *their* child.

They did what they could, sending him to counseling, practicing
tough love, calling the police a few times when it was warranted.
The mom talked to me and other teachers to let us know what was
going on. I tried to see beyond Brian's oppositional demeanor, letting him know he had worth and value, even when he messed up.

Both he and his parents persevered through his senior year. Brian's risky behavior diminished. He completed his required classes
and graduated. On the outside, he looked like just another kid
getting a diploma. But those of us who knew how close he had

51

been to dropping out or getting arrested knew how significant this milestone was.

Many parents have similar stories. Your kids make choices and have experiences you never anticipated. Each teen and young adult has a journey all their own. During the teen and young adult years, keeping your eyes on the long-term objectives we looked at in chapter 3 is essential. These goals keep you focused when reality distracts you. You're parenting to build skills, ethics, faith, and integrity for a lifetime, not just for now. Just as it's important to cast a vision, you need a strategy to get there.

Why? Because at times you only see what's in front of you and forget to see your child as the person she is becoming. You see her in her immaturity, immorality, disrespect, moodiness, or bad choices. Without looking forward, you feel bound by circumstances. Your reactions are driven by immediate needs rather than long-term objectives. You get weary, wanting to give up instead of pulling on God's strength for what's needed to get your child to the life God has for her.

Each of our kids is created in God's image, and God has a unique plan for them. You've already established a well-rounded vision for *each* of your kids in the last chapter, so let's look at God's plan for raising kids and letting them go by diving deeper into Psalm 127.

Three biblical principles from this psalm give us God's game plan for raising kids. These become *our* vision and strategy as Christian parents. Our kids need *us* to be focused on Jesus all the way to graduation and into their adulthood. They need us to be involved, active, and engaged with Jesus *and* with them for the entire journey.

PRINCIPLE AND STRATEGY #1 | *Children are a heritage . . . and parents establish the Christian foundation on which they stand.* A person's legacy lasts for generations to come, yet it's formed by what one lives day in and day out. The type of heritage a person leaves can be either positive or negative, healthy or unhealthy. How we invest in our children influences their heritage. Can you think of people in your family or church who left godly, positive, life-giving legacies upon their death? Can you also think of those who left a destructive heritage? I can. It's heartbreaking when unhealthy, toxic behavior is passed on from one generation to another.

Isaiah 43:7 says God formed and made each of us and that we are created for his glory. As Christian parents, we are called to raise our children with a foundation for a godly heritage, one that will glorify Christ. It won't happen without Jesus at the center of our efforts and our home. Remember—our labor is in vain unless Christ builds the home.

Contrary to popular belief, it's not your responsibility to raise godly kids. It's your responsibility to be a godly parent. A friend shared this perspective with me and it stuck. Too often we think we must produce a Christian prototype at age eighteen. This perception distracts us from the calling of being godly parents who position kids toward Jesus, with hearts open to him.

Godly parenting involves nurturing *your* relationship with Christ as your first priority, even over your relationship with your kids or spouse. This priority gets lost in the busyness of work, church, sports, laundry, and everything else you and your kids are involved in during the childrearing years.

It happened to me. For many years, I was a youth leader, Sunday school teacher, and Bible school teacher on top of being a mentor to my students. At the same time, I was critical and reactionary with my own kids. Children watch us and make judgments based on what they see. The Holy Spirit began convicting me about my hypocritical behavior. I was particularly convicted after an argument in which I said hurtful things to my teen and needed to ask for forgiveness. I decided to write a letter to my child, which brought about further conviction. My request for forgiveness included blame: "I shouldn't have said what I did, but when you . . ." I wrote and rewrote the apology three times before it was free of blaming statements. I had to be responsible for my own sinful and selfish behavior regardless of my child's actions.

I was the adult. The parent. I needed to own up to my ungodly behavior. It was one of the most humbling experiences of my life.

I put the letter on my teenager's bed. The next day, my teen came to me saying, "Mom, I got your note. I forgive you."

I had been a Christian since childhood, but I never truly knew grace until that moment. I did not deserve forgiveness, but my child extended it to me. And so did Jesus.

That was the first step of changing the tide of conflict and strife in our home. In order for me to leave a heritage reflecting Christ, *I* had to reflect him. To prepare my children's hearts to be open to God, I couldn't impose my rights or sinful behavior on them. It was damaging to our family and the faith I was professing in front of them.

However, when you surrender yourself to the Lord, he works in your life and that of your family. I believe this to my core because I've lived it.

Your behavior positively or negatively affects your family. Parenting in my own efforts brought strife and conflict. It was sobering to see the heritage I was leaving during that time.

What we live in front of our kids is the imprint we leave on their lives. How you respond, the standards you set, and the relationships you build with them are the places where your legacy takes root.

Take a moment to honestly consider what legacy you are currently leaving your children. See the first question under "Building up and letting go" to guide you.

PRINCIPLE AND STRATEGY #2 | *Offspring are a precious reward from God . . . a reward requiring hard work.* The most valuable rewards are those for which effort has been put forth, when you've worked hard and savor the sweetness of victory. But not every reward has equal value. An A on an exam means more when you overcome obstacles to obtain it. On the other hand, trophies received with no effort are cheap rewards.

Raising children is similar. The story at the beginning of the chapter is an example. Some kids get through childhood and adolescence fairly easily, but they are the minority in today's culture. There are more social, emotional, behavioral, and academic obstacles for kids to overcome in order to graduate and reach a healthy adulthood. Both teens and young adults are experiencing more adversity than past generations did. Consider a list of things with which so many youth struggle:

- depression
- suicidal ideation
- anxiety
- pornography use
- addiction
- isolation
- sexual assault
- peer pressure
- bad relationships
- isolation
- abuse
- bullying
- toxic parenting
- mental health issues

This is just a brief list of what young people may face. Many teens have experienced so much by the time they're eighteen, they feel they've already lived a lifetime.

This is true for kids raised in Christian homes, too. Remove assumptions that your kids will make it through high school or young adulthood unscathed. (We'll talk about more about navigating hard issues in future chapters.) Having great kids looks easy. It's not. I've walked it myself and journeyed with too many friends, peers, and clients to be persuaded differently.

Persevering through hardships with your teen or young adult requires commitment and reliance on God. The reward is precious, though, when you make it to the other side. And you *will* make it.

People may never know the path you take and the battles you fight to get your family to the place of God's reward.

But *you* do. And God does.

And that's when the reward is the sweetest.

PRINCIPLE AND STRATEGY #3 | *Like arrows, children are to be launched . . . and it takes a warrior to do it.* Psalm 127 is accurate: it *does* take a warrior to release children. Warriors are protectors and fighters for those under their care because there are dangerous predators who want to harm those they're protecting. Have you thought of yourself as a warrior? The biblical image of it is not antithetical to being a nurturer; in its purest from, it's a picture of a protector or provider for the vulnerable.

Your kids need you to be their warrior during childhood, especially in adolescence, when battles rage in both the physical and spiritual realms. The enemy of God doesn't want Jesus to be glorified through you or your family. He doesn't want your children to be influencers in their generation or to use their gifts and talents for the calling Jesus has for them.

Like arrows in the hands of warriors, our kids need to be equipped and prepared for their God designed journey. God uniquely created their targeted destination, just as a warrior uniquely crafts an arrowhead. The target of an arrow determines how an arrowhead is formed, aimed, and let go. Those meant for large game are different from those used for smaller game. Those used for waterfowl are different from those used on land.

These differences are similar for your kids too. Each of your children has a distinct purpose as a created child of God, one entirely different from their siblings'. God has distinctly crafted their journey. Your job isn't to create it for her, but to develop her gifts, personality, and passion in a way that positions her toward Christ. Out of that relationship, God uses their uniqueness for his glory (Isaiah 43:7). God wants each of us, no matter our age, to use the skills and gifts he's given us to glorify him and draw others to Christ. How the world would be changed if we did that!

As a warrior, God will equip you for these tasks, providing strength and stamina as you let those arrows fly!

BUILDING UP
and letting go

Father, thank you for the special plan you have for each of my children. Thank you for being with each of them throughout their life journey, even when I don't see the results. Help me to keep my eyes on the long-term perspective when immediate circumstances distract me from you and make me want to lose hope or give up. Amen.

1. What words describe the family heritage you would like to leave for your family?

2. Are there obstacles standing in the way? If so, what are they? What needs to change?

3. In what ways do you see yourself being a protector or provider for your kids as you prepare to let them go?

4. What is one principle you can apply to your family right now?

5

A Place Called Home

Therefore everyone who hears these words of mine and puts them into practice is like a wise man who built his house on the rock. The rain came down, the streams rose, and the winds blew and beat against that house; yet it did not fall, because it had its foundation on the rock.
—MATTHEW 7:24-25

"I just want to be *home*," Drew said on the other end of the phone. I've heard this sentence several times from my college kids. Sometimes it is said through tears, and other times it's spoken out of sheer exhaustion. Still other times it comes out of the mouth of a kid who just needs to talk to their mom or dad.

Home means a lot of things to different people. For most of us, home is where we grew up. My dad's parents were immigrants from Sicily and his home was a small, 668 square-foot house in what was at the time a middle-class neighborhood in the city of Gary, Indiana. We recently took our kids there to find their grandparents' childhood homes to connect them with their heritage. When we found my dad's house, it was uninhabited and the windows were smashed. The siding was peeling, the lot was overgrown, and trash was all over the yard. It's no longer the home where my grandparents built their American dream.

My dad's home was a significant part of his story. It was a big deal for his immigrant parents to be homeowners in America. They left their homeland, culture, and family with hopes and dreams for their children to have better opportunities than they'd had.

Like my grandparents, you want a home where hopes and dreams for your family can be realized. Perhaps you scour Pinterest to find pictures of your dream house or the perfect interior design project. There's a perception that if your home looks a certain way, your family will be living, laughing, and loving well—living the Instagram life.

Real life doesn't happen that way. You can stage the dreamy bliss, but it doesn't mean it exists. In a busy family with teens and young adults, your home likely has an empty refrigerator, smelly gym bags, half-completed home improvement projects, and arguing kids. And family dinnertime? Finding a mealtime where we're all home is rare.

A hectic life is what you have during the releasing years. Home is loud and chaotic, with a revolving door of people whose lives are dictated by the calendar. Most days, the only common denominator is where you all sleep at night.

Does that sound like your home?

Casting the vision for your family isn't just applicable to where they'll land when they leave, it's also about creating an environment they long to come back to. Home is where we long to feel known and accepted. We need home to be warm, secure, loving, and peaceful.

This type of home isn't created from the home décor aisles at Target: it's created from the climate *within* the home. Before we consider the varying aspects of nudging our children from the nest, we have to address the home itself: the spiritual foundation, the relationships within, and how home prepares kids for the world outside its doors.

A HOUSE THAT STANDS IN THE STORM | Jesus had important words about house and home.

> Therefore everyone who hears these words of mine and puts them into practice is like a wise man who built his house on the rock. The rain came down, the streams rose, and the winds blew and beat against that house; yet it did not fall, because it had its foundation on the rock. But everyone who hears these words of mine and does not put them into practice is like a foolish man who built his house on sand. The rain came down, the streams rose, and the winds blew and beat against that house, and it fell with a great crash. (Matthew 7:24-27)

Real life *is* stormy. One of my adult friends described home as the place she retreats after doing battle all day. If we feel that way about home and life as adults, imagine how it feels for a teen to go into a battle zone at school, online, and with peers every day. Teens aren't fully equipped to handle all the storms that rage around them. A place of retreat for teens and young adults is essential.

In prior generations, home was where kids felt safe from school and peer pressure. But your kid's battle just isn't "out there" anymore. Stress and pressure from the outside world is now with them wherever they go—whenever they have their phone, tablet, or the newest WiFi-enabled technology. People have access to them any time of day, even in the safety of home. Secret apps, video games, and social media connect them with peers and strangers who can stalk, intimidate, blackmail, and harm them. This is the new cultural normal for your kids, and it's ever changing. You and I must be engaged because home no longer shelters them from outside influences beyond our reach.

Creating a safe place for kids involves building your children's moral, intellectual, and emotional compass so they can make healthy decisions when you're not around. It involves building safety mechanisms inside them so internal alarms go off when something doesn't feel right. That's why relationship parenting is critical.

A safe home means *you* are safe to approach when kids need someone to talk to. Bullying, predators, dating violence, sexual assault, and exploitation are real risks for youth and young adults. Your kids need to know they can talk to you about these things. Relationship parenting makes you approachable and also builds the bridge for setting boundaries with social media, technology, and other things.

Technology is good because it connects our kids with others, thus fulfilling the need to belong, be affirmed, and be connected. Yet social media, chatrooms, and private messages can be harmful to kids because they're secretive, void of guidance, and often anonymous. They also replace face-to-face conversations and relationships, making our culture more disconnected. This relational disconnect is happening so rapidly we don't yet know the full implications of an entire generation being socialized this way.

Because of this, home needs to be emotionally safe for kids. They need a place of genuine connection within their family, where they can be their awkward, insecure, and sometimes disagreeable selves with unconditional love while they try to figure themselves out.

This safe climate happens not only through relationships, but also through internal and external boundaries. Helping your kids create internal boundaries is one of the healthiest gifts you can give to them, because those boundaries will keep them safe wherever they go. The security of boundaries through a loving relationship tells your children it's okay to come to you for help when they need it.

Yet many teens and young adults are afraid to talk to parents about the secret areas of their lives. This fear prevents them from reaching out when they really need help, when someone has harmed them, or if they have done something wrong. They're afraid of your response or what you will think of them.

Authentic relationships dispel this fear and make you more approachable about hurtful or harmful things. Kids need you, even though they won't come out and tell you. Instead, they test the waters to see how you respond. They want to know if it's okay to let you into their world, and if you're a safe place to land when storms rage around them. When girded with the strength and security of home, their wings are stronger for the rough life around them.

CLEANING HOUSE | Sometimes, however, storms erupt within the home. A toxic or rebellious child affects siblings, as do family members who are abusive or have addictions. Your own insecurities, bad habits, and hurts also affect your kids. Avoiding or ignoring these behaviors doesn't help. I've shared my angry, stressed-out, reactionary mom story and how my behavior negatively affected my family. Our family climate didn't change until I dealt with what *I* needed to change. Since then, I've worked with a lot of kids as a school counselor and therapist. I can tell you that unhealthy stuff in the lives of parents and siblings affects kids.

Are you ignoring sin, hurt, insecurities, or unhealthy behavior in your own life? Do you hide behind busyness, work, or your kids' activities so you don't have to face these things? Even if you think these things aren't affecting your home, they likely are in some way.

Before I dealt with my anger, I had another issue to deal with. From the time I was fourteen until my early twenties, I had an eating disorder. When Jenna was born, I realized I couldn't raise her with a healthy self-image if I didn't have a positive image of myself. I had to develop healthier thinking and behavior if I was going to raise a girl with an appropriate body image. I had to take care of my own stuff.

It's tempting to say, "But I can't be perfect. It's okay to be a mess. God loves me just the way I am, right?" Yes, God does love you the way you are and doesn't expect perfection. He cares about our needs, struggles, and wounds. But God also calls you and me to godliness and a healthy life. If you have sin or unresolved pain hindering the emotional health of your family, you need to deal with it.

Your family's health is also damaged when abusive or toxic behavior from a spouse, older siblings, or extended family members is present in the home. Kids are hurt by toxic people.

If these things are in your home, God needs to do some house-cleaning. Don't try to tackle these things yourselves. Seek profes-sional help when needed. Build a community of support. Enlist the strength and transforming power of Christ.

THE UNSEEN ENEMY OF HOME | Cleaning your house of unhealthy and toxic behavior is critical because there's an enemy who wants to destroy your family. Two verses are visual remind-ers of the unseen enemy of our homes. Ephesians 6:10-12 says, "Finally, be strong in the Lord and in his mighty power. Put on the full armor of God, so you can take your stand against the devil's schemes. For our struggle is not against flesh and blood, but against the rulers, against the authorities, against the powers of this dark world and against the spiritual forces of evil in the heavily realms." In 1 Peter 5:8-9, the apostle says, "Your enemy the devil prowls around like a roaring lion looking for someone to devour. Resist him, standing firm in the faith."

The devil is sneaky and deceitful. He scopes you out as the leader of your family, finds your weaknesses, and attacks in those areas. Satan lies to you by saying godliness is irrelevant and that your kids won't be accepted, successful, or happy if they follow an archaic faith built on Jesus Christ. He wants to devour and destroy your faith, your marriage, and your family.

But you are a warrior. Warriors need protection and weap-ons both defensively and offensively. God has armor specifically designed for you:

> Therefore put on the full armor of God, so that when the day of evil comes, you may be able to stand your ground, and after you have done everything, to stand. Stand firm then, with the belt of truth buckled around your waist, with the breastplate of righteousness in place, and with your feet fitted with the readi-ness that comes from the gospel of peace. In addition to all of this, take up the shield of faith, with which you can extinguish all the flaming arrows of the evil one. Take the helmet of sal-vation and the sword of the Spirit, which is the word of God. And pray in the Spirit on all occasions with all kind of prayers

and requests. With this in mind, be alert and always keep on praying for all the Lord's people. (Ephesians 6:13-18)

While there *is* a spiritual battle going on behind the scenes of your family, Christ is the victor because of his death and resurrection. If you feel your home or family is under attack, have hope! His name is Jesus.

You *can* walk through anything your family is facing. If the Lord has convicted you of an area you need to change, confess it to him and ask his forgiveness. First John 1:9 says when we confess our sins, Jesus is faithful and just and will forgive us our sins and clean us from all unrighteousness. Receive his forgiveness, then walk in the power of the Holy Spirit, allowing the Spirit to lead your family. He will do so because God *is* faithful. I've lived it.

Remember those words from Joel 2:25 I've referred to—about God restoring the years the locusts have eaten? That promise for Israel came after God called them to repentance. God's faithfulness of redeeming the years is a promise tied to confession, repentance, and obedience. When you walk obediently with Christ, you won't be saved from life's storms, but your house—and family— will stand.

A PLACE TO COME HOME TO | Your home is not only the place where kids grow up and where you prepare them for flight. It's also the place you hope they'll come back to. I recently talked with a mom whose two adult children flew far from the nest. Through tears, she told me how they rarely come home. Then she shared her grief and regret over different events that happened while she raised them. Listening to her, I realized the goal of childrearing is not just moving kids out, but also developing a climate at home to which kids want to return. Your family culture develops during the growing-up years, and you're often too busy or distracted to realize it.

Young adults leaving the nest also need a home base and a safe place to land. Home is still an important place of love, nurture, and constancy after they leave. Today's society is more mobile than ever before, and young adults are exploring more diverse opportunities than those in past generations, even well into their early thirties. Their relationships, jobs, and experiences are more transient than before. They still need the emotional connection of familiarity, warmth, and stability a childhood home provides, especially when they are in college or afterward.

Once your young adults have left, you might be ready to get rid of their stuff, downsize, or move to a different location. Do it with consideration or input from any young adults who are in transition, because home and the physical things inside the home may have significant meaning to them.

Believe me. I learned the hard way.

You may think your kids don't care about the physical surroundings of their childhood home, but certain things have intrinsic meaning and are a source of stability and familiarity in time of uncertainty. Emotional and mental health needs often arise among young adults during the college years or when they are in transition. It may be disarming and destabilizing if the physical surroundings of home are radically changed after they leave without them knowing or having input. Talk with young adults about significant changes you may make in your home or lifestyle, especially to their personal items or spaces. Ask them what they need from home when they come back on weekends or holidays. For some kids, this may really be important.

OUR HEAVENLY HOME | A chapter on home and your child's future wouldn't be complete without considering the most important home—our eternal home. In John 14:2, Jesus says, "In my Father's house are many mansions: if it were not so, I would have told you. I go to prepare a place for you" (KJV). Jesus also says there are two eternal resting places—heaven and hell (Matthew 25:46). Yet it's not popular or comfortable to talk about the eternal home separate from God, which is the consequence of sin and rejection of Jesus Christ.

Heaven as your eternal home only happens through a personal relationship with Jesus Christ, according to John 14:6. Jesus came to build relationships with each of us so we can have an eternal home with him in heaven. Ecclesiastes 3:11 says God sets eternity in our hearts. God created a longing within each of us for a heavenly home with him. Our privilege as Christian parents is to position our children's hearts so they will long for that home and the relationship that satisfies all longings—one with Jesus Christ.

You're not just building a home from which your kids will fly and to which they will sometimes return; you're building relationships for eternity. As already mentioned, the enemy wants to snatch your children and make them sons and daughters of this earth, not of God. Investing in the safe, secure climate of home and the relationships within it goes far beyond making children happy and healthy. It puts a longing in their souls for their eternal home of security and belonging.

Your kids won't find safety and security in this stormy place called earth; they will find it through a relationship with Jesus Christ. Do your best to prepare and position them; then trust the results to God.

BUILDING UP
and letting go

Lord, thank you for being the complete representation of home. Thank you for preparing a place for each of my children in your eternal mansion. Thank you for the home you're building within our family, though we may be scattered. Equip our home to be a place where each child feels safe and where each person belongs. Help me to deal with any sin or behavior I need to change to be a healthy presence and example in our family. Amen.

1. How would you describe the climate of your home? Take a moment to ask your kids for their description of home.

2. Do you feel home is emotionally safe for each of your kids right now? If not, what areas can be improved?

3. Are there areas in your life that are hindering the family climate or negatively affecting one or more of your kids? If so, what can you do to change that?

6

Build Family Ties

A cord of three strands is not quickly broken.
—ECCLESIASTES 4:12

"Mom, he's being a jerk!" one of my kids said about another sibling. They often don't rat each other out. When they do, I pay attention.

Do your kids fight? Mine do. It's normal. It can also drive a parent crazy. It hurts to see those you love not getting along.

The climate of the home isn't just bound to the *place* your kids call home; it includes the *relationships* formed there. What happens among siblings and parents during the growing-up years forms the family ties that kids take into adulthood. These lifelong relationships make up the family.

Family roots grow deep during these crazy years when everyone is home. The family is where kids are first socialized. It's where they learn about love, acceptance, safety, conflict, giving, and taking. Kids can love and hate each other all in the same day. Does your family life seem like the worst reality TV show some days? Does sibling conflict spill down the family food chain from oldest to youngest?

It's happened at our house. Some days you feel you've done nothing right as a parent, and you fear your kids will be at odds with each other forever. Many times I've projected how their adult relationships will be on the basis of how they treat each other in the moment. That's scary!

But then I bring myself back to reality and look honestly at the state of relationships within the home. Several descriptions of home from the previous chapter express what siblings need from one another and from us as parents.

"Home is where I know and feel I belong" was a comment I heard from someone about home. I love this description. Belonging somewhere is a longing of every human. A home where each member belongs is a place where family members feel safe with one another, especially among siblings. Siblings *become home* for each other when kids scatter, parents move, the childhood home is no longer, and eventually when we, the parents, die.

Strong, healthy bonds keep your family together as kids go their separate ways. How do you build those family ties while you are simultaneously loosening the strings for the fledging season?

WE ARE A FAMILY | Unfortunately, family ties are often strained by sibling rivalry, individual needs, jealousy, personality differences, and favoritism. Scripture is full of unhealthy sibling relationships, including the first two children, brothers Cain and Abel (Genesis 4). Their relationship was filled with jealousy and hatred. It ended in death. The Bible records other stories of sibling strife, which shows that God cares about family relationships, including what goes on in your home.

Sibling relationships are important to God because family is his model for community and care. Psalm 68:6 says, "God sets the lonely in families." God uses family as the first and primary place in which to foster a sense of belonging and being known, accepted, and loved. Yet many kids grow up feeling lonely or alone within their families. A young adult once told me how he felt completely alone in a family of six. God places the lonely in families; he doesn't intend for those within families to feel alone.

What makes a child feel alone when surrounded by parents and siblings? Words like "I hate you!" "You're so stupid!" "I wish you were never born."

It grieves a mother's heart to hear words like this spoken between her children. You love each of them completely and unconditionally, no matter their faults. It hurts when there's animosity between them. I can only imagine Eve's pain when one of her children killed another. That's mom pain none of us want to experience.

Yet some siblings frequently spew harmful and reckless words. Jesus says hateful thoughts and words are the same as committing murder (Matthew 5:21-25). It's crucial that fathers and mothers pay attention to sibling dynamics. Younger siblings can be targeted by older teens and young adults. They can be overlooked or made to feel small and unimportant. The moods, behavior, and language of adolescent siblings can intimidate and hurt younger ones.

Observe sibling relationships, being aware that bullying behavior can happen in families. Bullying occurs when there's an imbalance of power and when someone harms another person on purpose, repeatedly, and over time. It usually happens out of a parent's sight. The targeted sibling usually feels alone, voiceless, or intimidated. In the past, when one of my kids has crossed the line between normal teasing and hurtful behavior, another sibling has told me about it because it bothers him or her. That's when I know normal strife is ramping up.

Sibling strife is normal; hatred and animosity is not. It's our job to set the standard for sibling behavior and to hold kids accountable. Addressing sibling strife can be done by saying, "We are a family. You may not like your sister right now, but you are expected to honor her." Other times, confrontation might have to be more direct.

Sibling relationships are lifetime relationships; enforcing these standards is important. The good news is family dynamics usually change when a moody teen moves out or goes to college. The younger sibling has space to be his own person. Both siblings grow up, and relationships often get better.

However, more difficult circumstances don't just fade away. Kids who are toxic or rebellious or who have untreated mental health issues or an addiction deeply affect others in the family, regardless of whether that child lives in the home. A younger sibling may act out, withdraw, or struggle when living in the shadow of a toxic sibling. While you can't control an adult child's behavior, helping and protecting younger siblings *is* within your realm. However, a younger child may be the one negatively affecting the family. If these situations are present in your family, seek support and help, not just for the toxic child but for the whole family.

God is with your family, no matter how rough it is. God answered Eve's pain by showing extraordinary mercy to her family. Genesis 4 tells us God put a mark of protection on Cain, the murderous son, and gave Eve another child to replace the one she lost. God was still the author of their family and is the author of *your* family too. Do you need that hope?

Take your concerns about sibling relationships to God. Ask the Holy Spirit for wisdom to see things objectively without showing favoritism. Is the conflict situational, or is there something deeper? Seek God's discernment for how to handle it. Then, build up relationships during nonconflict times.

Focus on God's sovereignty and presence, praising God for what he *is* doing among your children, though you may not see it. With Christ as the foundation, your home *will* withstand the storm. The sun will eventually come out and shine on your family.

AS FOR ME AND MY HOUSE | Even if the preceding situations aren't true of your family, the changes and transitions of the releasing years are naturally difficult on relationships. You have to be vigilant and creative to keep the family connected. Raising independent adults means you don't know when the whole family will be together again for holidays, important events, or vacations. This has been our struggle, with college kids who work and have summer internships, plus the revolving door of high school activities and kids living away from home. Here are a few suggestions for keeping the family connected during this season of change:

1. Do things with all siblings present as much as possible, being realistic and not legalistic. If your kids are all still home, choose one meal or another weekly time where everyone can be together. Be creative. One family I know had breakfast together a couple of times a week because it was the only time everyone was home. When vacations or holidays are difficult to coordinate with everyone's schedules, focus on the time you're together rather than the ideal event. The last summer all my children were home, we couldn't find one full day where everyone's schedules meshed. We had to drastically change the plans I hoped for. I had to be okay with simply being together instead of having the dream getaway.

    I've often told my kids I don't care when we get together; it's just important we are. Just be together. Sometime. Any time.

2. Celebrate with each other. As much as possible, include everyone for big celebrations. This goes beyond birthdays. Celebrate significant accomplishments in each other's lives, no matter how young or old the siblings are. When older siblings can't be there, use live streaming technology to connect. Communicate positive happenings in each other's lives. Encourage older siblings who have moved out to connect and spend time with younger siblings who are "left behind."

3. Develop a family culture. Family traditions, work, and activities define your family culture. What are things that make your family unique? If you don't know, ask your kids. We are notorious for having at least one disastrous day on family vacations. Though horrible in the moment, these days are now humorous memories that bind our family together.

    Family culture is also the answer to "why" questions. Surly teens may ask, "Why do we have to do this?" or "Why do I have to get along with him?" Your answer can simply be, "Because we're a family and we love each other." This response is especially necessary for sibling strife we've talked about.

4. Foster a climate of compassion, respect, and grace for one another. That sense of belonging each of us has? Your kids crave that within the family. Set expectations of honor and respect. When siblings have conflict, avoid taking sides, but hold each one accountable. When possible, share a compassionate perspective to one sibling about the other, but don't force a sibling to "understand" where another is coming from. Validate your children's feelings even if you don't agree with their perspective. And when you're not sure how to respond, give grace. I've had to do this several times.

5. Let siblings work things out between themselves. A few years ago, as Ron and I prepared to teach a parenting class, I asked Drew and Mark what they thought would be helpful tips for younger parents. They both said, "You and Dad let us work things out."

    Kids need to figure out how to work through conflict and get along with people they don't agree with. They'll need these skills in the workplace and in other relationships. Sibling relationships are where these skills first start. However, when strife is harmful, take action as mentioned earlier.

6. Place Christ as the center of your family. Ecclesiastes 4:12 says, "A chord of three is not quickly broken." This verse places Christ as the unbreakable element in relationships. Jesus holds a family together despite obstacles, pain, or brokenness because he is what strengthens, protects, and secures. There's a chapter on prayer coming up that lays the foundation, with Christ as the binding unit within your family.

BLESSED BE THE TIES THAT BIND | Family ties keep the family together past the growing-up years, leaving the heritage Psalm 127 talks about. Our family has been privileged to experience a strong, godly legacy firsthand.

My father-in-law passed away from kidney failure during the writing of this book. We knew death was eminent when his body became too frail to withstand any more dialysis treatments. Ron and I called our children and told them if they wanted to see Grandpa, they probably should come soon.

During his final days, all twelve of his grandchildren were able to say goodbye to him. The grandkids ranged in age from sixteen to thirty-eight. One particular evening, ten of them were gathered together with him around his hospital bed. They laughed, cried, and shared memories with Grandpa about the days they ran around on the farm. Growing up on the farm allowed the grandchildren innumerable opportunities to spend time with Grandpa doing ordinary things that grew strong roots.

Then, it was Grandpa's turn to say his goodbyes. He knew each of his kids, grandkids, and great-grandkids intimately, and he spoke to each one as an individual. He made it a practice to be involved with each one as much as he could, attending their events, asking about their interests, and investing time with them.

He finished that particular evening by praying a blessing over each grandchild and over each of his four sons and daughters-in-law. He petitioned God with his last desires for his family before he went home to be with Jesus. He hung on a few days more until the last grandchild could be there and he could say his last goodbye. We witnessed the tangible meaning of a home, heritage, and a family legacy built by Christ in those moments. For each of his sons and grandchildren, Grandpa himself was *home*. He was safe and secure; he offered understanding and freedom. He built a family where roots, faith, and love run deep.

Family is God's gift. A home that *God* builds withstands storms and leaves a heritage reflecting the heavenly Father and his goodness for generations to come. Family ties, rooted in Jesus, live on after we do.

BUILDING UP
and letting go

Lord, thank you for each of my kids. Help me to have your perspective when I see my kids fight. Give me strength to confront them and hold them accountable, and also wisdom for when to let things go. Thank you for being the author of my family. Amen.

1. What current frustrations do you have with your kids and their relationships with one another?

2. What do you think might be the root of the strife?

3. How can you build family ties within your family right now?

4. What's one principle in this chapter to act on?

7

Growing Pains

So neither the one who plants nor the one who waters is anything, but only God, who makes things grow.
—1 CORINTHIANS 3:7

When Jenna went to college for the first time, we all crammed in the van and moved her to a university eleven hours away from home. It was a family affair. When it was time to say goodbye, she clung to her dad and said, "I don't want you guys to go." They stood there, hugging, for a long time. The rest of us awkwardly stood there in silence.

Thankfully, the siblings weren't as emotionally charged as the parents. The sixteen-year-old said, "This is when we get in the van and drive away."

We were brought back to the reality that goodbyes have to be said, kids have to grow up, and families have to change.

It's called growing pains. And sometimes it stinks.

As each child leaves, the family changes. Within a few months, I got used to Jenna being gone. There were still three boys at home: in high school, middle school, and elementary school. When Mark left for college three years later, it was much different. There was a loud quietness with just two kids under our roof. There were also changes in the pecking order. Drew, the middle boy, had a new confidence. He liked the role of being the oldest in the house. He and Ethan learned to get along better if they wanted someone to do something with because it was just the two of them.

We got used to being a family of four. We didn't have to cram into a vehicle, and we ate out more frequently. Each child got his voice heard, in some ways for the first time.

Three years later, we are a family of three. One evening our youngest said, "Sometimes I really miss one of my siblings being around."

I said, "I do too." We both shed tears.

Growing pains are real when kids leave. Growing *through* the changes is critical.

WHY CHANGE NEEDS TO HAPPEN | I got a text message from one of the college kids informing me that Drew was watching a reportedly "raunchy" movie because of a tweet Drew posted. I texted back, letting the college kid know I was aware of the movie. In fact, his dad and I were watching it with him.

I let the informer know the "little boys" weren't so little anymore.

Older siblings often see younger ones through the lens of when they were home. It took Jenna a few years to realize her "baby brothers" weren't ten and twelve anymore like they were when she went to college.

The first time one of our younger kids stood up for himself to a sibling in college, it was a surprise! He realized he didn't have to do what his older sibling told him to do anymore, and said so. It was a healthy transition.

I learned about the importance of these changes through my own family experience. As the youngest in my family of origin, I developed a voice and an identity when my older sisters went to college. Unfortunately, our sibling roles didn't shift as our family changed. At fourteen, I longed to be treated as an equal by my older siblings instead of being seen as the "baby." The circumstances triggered the onset of anorexia. Though other factors contributed to my eating disorder, my role in the family was intricately tied to it.

Family dynamics affect each child, and it's important a family grows with the changes.

BIRTH ORDER | Do the following statements sound familiar to you? Firstborns like to be in charge. Middle kids are the quiet peacemakers or the troubled children. Youngest kids are spoiled, the "baby," or the family clown.

Birth order stereotypes contain bits of truth. As the oldest sibling, firstborns tend to take on more responsibility and leadership. They often feel responsible for the family. If there's a middle child (or children), this kid often is the peacemaker who tries to diffuse conflict between other siblings. However, middle kids sometimes have to fight for their voice in the family, causing them to either be quiet or at odds with parents and siblings as they fight for their position. A lastborn child can be seen by older siblings as the baby who never grows up or who is spoiled. Sometimes the youngest is the family clown who seeks attention as she grows out of the cute stage.

Birth order influences families.[1] As your family grows and changes, family *roles* should also change. Help each of your kids find their unique identity outside of their birth order. Foster fairness, individuality, honor, and respect. With each child who leaves the nest, give the next child the opportunity to lead. Give her similar expectations and opportunities her siblings had at their ages. When adult children interact with younger siblings, foster equality rather than the childhood pecking order.

You may have felt like you've failed in this area. Many parents wish they would have parented differently with their older kids, especially their firstborn. I'm one of them. God gives us kids when we're immature and inexperienced. You may have shown favoritism, partiality, or unfair treatment to one of your kids. You may

---

1. Author Kevin Leman has written books that go into deeper dynamics on birth order and how it affects personality, worldview, and development. These include *The Birth Order Book* and *The Firstborn Advantage*.

have been critical of a child whose personality or temperament challenges you. Confess it, accept it, but don't stay stuck in regret.

God is bigger than your mistakes and mine; he's more powerful than your sin and mine. God redeems the pain of the past because he is faithful.

THE REVOLVING DOOR | It was kind of nice for the first several weeks when just Drew and Ethan were home after Mark left for college. There were fewer loads of laundry. The housework was easier. Groceries lasted longer. I was a little more organized and a little less frazzled.

After taking care of four kids, I felt as if I were on vacation. Just taking care of two seemed easy.

The bliss lasted about three weeks. Then the whirlwind started. Mark came home every few weekends to see his girlfriend, Samantha, who was in high school. Both college students had different school breaks; during the summer they had different work schedules. Jenna had internships and classes abroad. I didn't know who was coming or going. There were shoes everywhere, the refrigerator was empty, and I couldn't keep track of everyone's schedules. When I asked the college kids about their schedules, I got the "I don't check in with you at school; why do I need to at home?" response.

There's a revolving door when college kids or young adults come and go while you still have kids at home. They want their independence, but they're still under your roof part of the time. They share spaces with the family, and there are still house rules they have to follow.

There can be tension and conflict. College kids are surprised when younger siblings take over space that used to be theirs. They wonder why things are different, including you. "What happened to my parents?" our older kids have said on more than one occasion after leaving for college. With fewer kids at home, our family environment shifted. Ron and I developed new hobbies and interests, including a dog I never thought I'd have.

Once that first child leaves, things are never quite the same. Your kids grow and change, but you do too. It's something you love and hate all at the same time.

So how do you navigate the revolving door of change with young adults and younger kids and still keep your sanity? Here are a few tips.

SETTING EXPECTATIONS | You and your young adults probably have different expectations for college breaks or extended holidays. They've been on their own and have made their own decisions (hopefully!). It's an adjustment for them to move in with parents and siblings even for a few weeks. You don't know much about their personal life, and they don't know much about yours. They're coming home with their own experiences, needs, and expectations of home. More than likely, they won't tell you what their needs are.

As the parent, you've got your own expectations for when they move back for extended periods. You may or may not be excited for them to come home (come on, let's be honest). You may be torn between happiness at seeing them and anxiety about having your new normal disrupted. You may have discovered you get along with them better while they're away. These are just a few of the mixed feelings parents and young adults have during the college or post–high school years.

Consider the following questions as you think about realistic expectations for returning young adults:

- What expectations will there be about laundry and cleaning their bedroom, bathroom, and other shared or private spaces?
- What are expectations about shared spaces with other siblings?
- What expectations do you have about family chores, meals, and sleeping in?
- What expectations do you have about schedules, curfews, and friends coming over?

- What are expectations about jobs, cars, phones, personal items, and other financial areas?
- What expectations do you have about family events or activities with younger siblings?
- What are your expectations about church attendance and participation in extended family gatherings?
- What are expectations about possible moral differences—drinking, drug use, or sexual activity? These issues often arise.

These are common areas of conflict and frustration between parents and young adults. For us, guidelines revolve around independence and family responsibilities. When my kids are in college and come home, I expect them to take care of their personal things just as they do at school—laundry, for example. They're expected to respect the spaces we all use and to clean up after themselves. If they're going to be out late, they let us know where they'll be or who they'll be with both out of courtesy and for safety. These expectations flex with age. I have different expectations for a nineteen-year-old college student than for a twenty-one- or twenty-two-year-old.

They are also expected to follow family rules while home—holding down a job, helping with indoor and outdoor chores, getting up at a reasonable time. We ask them to respect the family morals we've set while they're at home. (We'll talk more about boundaries and responding to violations in later chapters.) These are some of our guidelines, but yours may be different.

When setting these expectations, it's reasonable to negotiate. Similar guidelines should be used if you have a young adult living at home full time. But don't treat them as if they are in high school, because they're not. They're adults. They, in turn, should respect the fact that living at home is a privilege, not a right.

You'll have challenges with your adult children that didn't exist when they were in high school. You'll also have different expectations for them than you do for your younger kids. The younger ones may not understand why their older siblings have more lenient rules. The older kids may think it's not fair if you've changed rules for their younger siblings. It's tempting to get pulled into arguments over these things. Don't. Focus on family *ties* rather than on what divides.

LEFT BEHIND | Being the youngest with older siblings coming and going is a unique position. The transition for this child may be difficult. Younger children with an age gap between them and older siblings can really struggle, especially if they are close to an older sibling or if there are only two children in the family. The younger sibling may experience his own form of grief as his world changes and he loses companions, mentors, and support. On the other hand, younger siblings may embrace the time they have with just their parents, especially if they've felt overshadowed by older siblings and their activities.

Older siblings grow up with people all around them, and the younger siblings get used to being by themselves. Your youngest's relationship with you will be different from your relationships with your older kids because of the time you have exclusively together. Some people say it's like raising a different family after the older ones leave.

This, too, is hard. It's another type of grief. Here are a few suggestions to keep in mind for this particular transition:

- Keep the family connected and involved in each other's lives as much as possible, even when siblings live far away.
- Spend time with your youngest, even though your schedule may be full. You're still parenting her. She needs you as much as the others did.
- Refrain from babying younger children or treating them differently than you would have treated their siblings at a particular age.
- Continue with family traditions, even if it's just the three of you left at home.
- If the youngest is having a hard time with an older sibling leaving, encourage the older one to stay connected, even if it's just through text messages or live video. Give them time together when everyone's home.

- Empathize with the youngest over the losses, but don't over-compensate. He will adjust. It'll just be different.
- Advocate for each child to see each other as individuals. Push your family to grow into adult roles of mutual respect and individuality. Continue to celebrate and share in each other's successes.
- Let your youngest have her high school life that's separate from her siblings' lives. Grandkids, weddings, or an older sibling's move across the country may happen when the youngest is still home. She shouldn't have to spend every vacation visiting an older siblings if she wants to hang out with her friends. It's tempting to put an older sibling's experiences ahead of the youngest's activities. But it's her time now. Help her live it with similar opportunities her siblings had.

The revolving-door years are full of transitions and growing pains. People come and go. Routines are disrupted. Relationships change. You may not have a new normal until all the kids are gone.

Which is, of course, the thing you dread most.

Grow with your family. Build family ties. Let some things go. And hold on to what's most important.

BUILDING UP
and letting go

*Father, thank you for my family even in the moments we feel the
most scattered. Thank you for the relationships we are building
even in the harried, hard moments. Equip each of my children to
respect and honor one another. Bless our family as we grow and
change through this stage. Amen.*

1. Do you see the roles your children take on within your
   family? List them here.

2. What can you do to foster strong relationships between
   your kids right now?

3. Do you find yourself babying your youngest? If so, how
   can you change that?

4. What's one principle you can currently apply to
   your family?

8

One and All

For God so loved the world that he gave his one and only Son, that whoever believes in him shall not perish but have eternal life.
—JOHN 3:16

"I won't be able to come," I told Ethan, our youngest. "Mark asked if I could be there for his race, and it's really important to him. I'm sorry."

It was one of many times we've had overlapping events in one day with multiple children.

Ethan, a high school sophomore, had a regional cross-country meet qualifying him for the next level of the state championship. Mark, a college senior, had organized a 5K road race with classmates to honor a college professor who died of cancer a few weeks earlier. The members of his education major cohort group were very close, and they were also close to their beloved professor. Mark talked about Mrs. Forrest and her cancer journey throughout his college experience, often asking us and our church to pray for her. She influenced him deeply. The race was the way he and his classmates wanted to celebrate and honor her.

Unfortunately, the 5K fell on the day of Ethan's race. Having missed Ethan's qualifying race the year before because of a speaking engagement, I had been planning to be there for him.

Then Mark called. Boys in college rarely call home, and this kid hardly asks for anything. "Mom, are you going to be at the race?" he asked.

"Yes," I said.

Ethan still had two more years of qualifying races, and his dad could be at this one. Mark would likely plan only one race in honor of a life-changing professor, and he specifically asked me to come. I knew where I needed to be.

THE FAMILY OR THE INDIVIDUAL | As a parent, you're a caregiver, and meeting the needs of others during this phase of life pulls you in different directions. If you have more than one child, you know the struggle of balancing the needs of two or more children. With multiple kids at different stages, we've had a lot of conflicting events. As kids get older, it's not just sporting events that collide. College graduations conflict with proms. Life events of older kids conflict with important events of younger siblings. On top of that, you may be taking care of your own aging parents, who need you in different ways. Lots of people need you, and it's hard to balance it all.

Knowing who needs you the most isn't in the parenting books. Discernment involves assessing the needs of the individual child along with the needs of the family. It doesn't end when kids leave home. In fact, it gets harder as kids scatter.

The day of Ethan's and Mark's races, Drew, a college freshman, also had his first basketball game as a college athlete. Looking at the schedule for the day, Ron and I realized the starting times of each event could possibly allow us to make it to all three. So we hustled the whole day and made it to all three events (though we broke the speed limit all over Indiana). It's just one of many times we did the best we could to be there for each child. It makes for crazy, busy days, but we've never regretted it. What's happening in the lives of *each* child is important to us.

It's also important to our children.

While God cares about the family unit, he also values the individual. Matthew 10:30 says even the hairs on your head are known by God. He is personal. Your heavenly Father *knows* you and sets the standard for parenting both the individual and the family.

TO BE KNOWN AND UNDERSTOOD | Kids need to feel individually known within the family, primarily by you, their parents. Feeling seen and known may be even more essential during the adolescent years. Though your teens may say to you, "You don't understand!" what they're really saying is, "I need you to understand me!" It's the longing we all have.

Being known makes us feel loved.

There's less strife between siblings when kids feel accepted and valued. When a teen or young adult knows you have her best interest at heart, it's easier for her to accept decisions that seem unfair. Ethan could have pointed out that I had missed his qualifying meet the year before. He could have said I had been there for all of Mark's high school events. But he was secure in our relationship. He knew I wasn't pushing him off because his race wasn't important. He understood why this race of Mark's was special. He had learned he didn't have to compete with his brother for love, acceptance, and support.

Jesus gave a beautiful example of how to handle relationships between siblings and what may seem to be unfair treatment. The prodigal son parable of Luke 15:11-32 tells of an older brother who was bothered by the treatment his rogue brother received. The big brother did what he was supposed to do, but his rebellious baby brother took an early inheritance and squandered it. When the playboy came home, their father threw him a party.

The older brother was mad. "'My son,' the father said, 'you are always with me, and everything I have is yours. But we had to celebrate and be glad, because this brother of yours was dead and is alive again; he was lost and is found!'" (Luke 15:31-32).

This story shows how much God loves *all* of us and yet values *each* of us.

In John 21:20-24, Jesus gave a similar response to Peter about his envy toward the apostle John. Peter asked, "Lord, what about him?" Jesus' response was, "What is that to you? You must follow me."

Ouch.

Have you ever wanted to say, "What's it to you?" when one of your kids says, "What about him?" I have. Most of us have at least one child whose world revolves around fairness, equality, and questions such as "What about him?" In essence, Jesus was telling Peter, "Don't worry about others. Do what I've asked, because I know what's best for you and I know what's best for them. I've got it covered."

Our kids need to hear these words when they envy or fixate on fairness. They want to trust that you have their best interest at heart. They need assurance that your love isn't something for which they have to compete. They want to know you have their back, even while you have the back of their sibling.

Your kids want equality and fairness, yet equality and fairness are different. Equal parenting can be legalistic, because you're not taking individual needs and other factors into consideration. Legalism leads to rebellion when it's absent of relationship, nurture, and love. Being fair, however, is a better principle to follow when you look at context and a child's age, behavior, maturity, and level of trust. More than equality, kids really want to know you're consistent and fair. Though older kids may disagree with decisions you make with younger siblings, they'll respect it more when they know you've got everyone's back and you value fairness.

Kids shouldn't have to jockey for a position in the family hierarchy of mom's and dad's favor. When everyone's place in the family is secure, there's peace. It's a beautiful gift for each of your kids to know they are loved, seen, and understood.

Knowing your kids as individuals is a conscious choice. It involves studying them, listening to them, and seeing their uniqueness. It's done by spending time with them one-on-one, which gets harder as each child leaves. During the years my kids have been home, I've tried to spend time with each child by going somewhere special with each of them during summer vacation. Once teens and college students are working, this "date" may just be going out to eat. Your younger kids? Take them with you when you are shopping or running errands. Spending time with kids doesn't have to be a major event you post about on social media. It can happen in the daily routines of life and still be special.

The effort, though, is important. One-on-one time makes your child feel loved and known. It builds your relationship with her. It's during these times your kids often share something important with you.

You may have to say no to other things to make it work. I volunteer less for Ethan's events than I did for his siblings' activities so I can visit the college kids when I have time. When schedules overlap, Ron and I split events so we can have meaningful times with each of the kids.

In a few years you won't have to go to any ball games or music concerts. You won't have time in the car to talk with your kids about what's going on in their lives. Getting to know your kids when they're living at home builds a lifetime relationship. Make time so you can listen to what they're *not* saying. When one of your kids is argumentative or disrespectful, there's usually more going on in her life than she is letting on.

Adolescents are trying to figure out a lot of stuff. Their behavior can often be offensive, ugly, and rude as they push you away. Yet when they act unlovable, it usually means they need you the most.

KEEPING A BALANCE | We had kids in high school, middle school, and older and younger elementary school for a long time. Then they were in college, high school, middle school, and elementary school. You're stretched when you have older kids' activities and younger ones with homework, practices, and an early bedtime. Unfortunately, busyness doesn't end as your kids get older.

Some of the best times in family life are also the most exhausting. Sporting events, milestones, important activities. Do you ever feel your schedule is out of control?

If so, focus on the goals you worked on in the beginning of this book. Without long-term, intrinsic objectives for your family, you get sucked into the whirlpool of busyness and what needs to be done today. When that happens, performance parenting ramps up rather than relationship parenting. Your kids will feel it, and they'll gravitate toward this climate of striving too. They'll jockey for position for who is best at things, who gets the most awards, and whose events are more important.

Your kids need balanced priorities and it starts with you and me. Are you pushing your kids to strive at unhealthy levels because you're afraid they won't be successful in sports, academics, college, or career? There's a new term among kids: FOMO, or fear of missing out. Beware of catering to this mentality. The world says busyness and activities equal success. It's a subtle lie the enemy wants you to believe.

That's the world's standard. But God's ways are not of this world. Romans 12:2 says, "Do not conform to the pattern of the world, but be transformed by the renewing of your mind. Then you will be able to test and approve what God's will is—his good, pleasing and perfect will."

We don't need to be sucked in by the pressures of the world. When your family is built on the foundation of Christ, you don't need to chase what the world chases and *how* they chase it. It'll be in vain.

Instead, seek God and his plan for your family and *each* of your children. God will guide your steps and the path your child walks. "Commit to the Lord whatever you do, and he will establish your plans," says Proverbs 16:3.

When seeking God's will for decisions, priorities, and financial commitments for your family, you can trust him with the outcomes. He will be faithful. Does it seem risky to consult God about family activities in the twenty-first century? It shouldn't. God knows your child's future. He cares about your teen's and young adult's activities, because he cares about them. Remember, God has a path for their lives. Encouraging your children to be busy because everyone else is or because you're afraid they'll miss out is faulty thinking.

If you follow Christ, you can trust him. But you have to walk in faith to see his provision.

Faith is not acting on your impulses, dreams, or assumptions. It's also not asking God to bless your worldly desires. Faith is seeking *him* first, following his lead, and trusting him with the results.

If, for a season, God is calling you to say no or to wait for a decision or activity for your kids, trust him. Commit your schedules, responsibilities, time, and priorities to the Lord. You will see him deliver.

I have. He does not fail.

AFFIRMATION AND ENCOURAGEMENT | First Corinthians 12:12-26 is the example of how everyone within the church has a unique and different role. Each one is valuable and needed to make the body function as a healthy unit. The same is true of your family. But competition, comparison, and jealousy are killers of family cohesiveness. Therefore, build up each of your kids with affirming words and actions. Let your kids know how valuable they are to the family. Talk with them about the particular role they play—not because of birth order but because of their personality and gifts.

Validate your kids' individual strengths. Encourage them to value each other for the gifts and uniqueness they bring to the family. Here are some practical tips for how to do this:

- Praise your kids often but privately as much as possible. Do it in the car, at bedtime, right after an event, or when you've caught them doing something good. Write them a note or text them when you think of them and how proud you are of them. I do this with my college kids, who usually think it's weird to get a random text in the middle of their day. I'm okay with being weird.
- Praise them for their character traits and not just their accomplishments. Exclusive praise for successes promotes performance- and works-based values. Affirm your kids for their nature and kindness and the unique traits you see in

them. Let them know how these attributes contribute in a positive way to the family.

- Affirm your kids *within* the family. On birthdays, each of us shares something positive about the person we're celebrating. It builds relationships among siblings, even those who don't get along all the time.

Encouraging words cost you nothing, but they build up your kids and bind your family together.

BUILDING UP
and letting go

Father, thank you for knowing each of my kids individually. Thank you for their uniqueness and what they contribute to our family. Help me to see the kids when they need to be seen and to hear what they're not saying. Bond our family together and build each child's strengths. Amen.

1. What are the challenges you face in spending time with your kids individually?

2. List your kids' names below and write down two or three things that define their uniqueness, gifts, or contributions to the family.

3. How can you affirm each of your children?

4. What principle can you apply to your family right now?

9

The Way
They Should Go

Start children off on the way they should go, and even when they are old they will not turn from it.
—PROVERBS 22:6

It was playtime at Jenna's preschool, and it was my first time as a helper mom in a school setting. The girls were playing dress-up and the boys were running around doing something loud. One girl was making a dramatic speech, and the kids around her were all laughing.

I looked around, wondering where Jenna was. Before long I found her in the reading corner; she was sitting on a chair and looking at books. I walked over to Jenna and asked her if she wanted to play with the other kids. She said no and continued reading.

Doubts crossed my mind. Why didn't she want to play with the other kids? She wasn't shy at home, so why wasn't she being social like the others?

That night, I told Ron my fears. Jenna wasn't playing with the main group of girls. She was by herself, reading books in a corner.

"What's wrong with that?" he asked.

Ron's response surprised me. He wasn't alarmed by her behavior at all. In fact, it's what he would have been doing at that age. Ron's response exposed my expectation that Jenna should act like me because she was a girl.

This was one of my first lightbulb moments as a mother. Jenna was my husband's child too. And she was not a mini-me.

Have you ever assumed your child, especially one who is the same gender as you are, would be like you? It's a natural expectation. Many parents have an underlying assumption that their children will simply be better versions of themselves. Seeing your child with different hopes, dreams, opinions, and interests can rock your world. It causes angst for a lot of parents.

Our kids are not our clones. If God had wanted two of us, he would have created two.

Our children's distinctive traits can make it hard to understand and parent them. But it's essential we foster our kids' individual gifts and strengths, which requires first recognizing they are autonomous and separate from us.

FINDING THEIR OWN WAY | "Train up a child in the way he should go," says Proverbs 22:6 (KJV); "and when he is old, he will not depart from it." This verse is the best model for *why* fostering your child's individual gifts, personality, and temperament is important. Children open their hearts to a relationship with their heavenly Father when they are intimately known and accepted by their earthly parents. Being in a home where their God-given skills, personalities, and temperaments are valued makes their souls tender for the love of Christ.

Nurture the unique ways God has created your child instead of making her conform to the person you think she should be. Sometimes we don't mean to mold her in our own image, but it happens.

From a young age, Ethan had different interests from those of his brothers. He was our Thomas the Tank Engine guy when the others were John Deere boys. He loved science. He didn't have interest in sports involving balls, but we still signed him up for the basketball league when he was young because his siblings had played.

It soon became apparent Ethan didn't have the ball ability his brothers had. When basketball registration forms came home one year, Ethan handed them to me with hunched shoulders.

His nonverbal cues told me clearly how he felt about basketball.

"Ethan, you don't have to play basketball," I told him.

"I don't?" he asked, with a mix of relief and excitement. Then he asked, "But what will Dad think?"

The question exposed the messages our kids get from us. I had to listen to what he wasn't saying.

I told him his dad would be fine with it. Ethan's shoulders straightened. A weight was lifted when he realized he didn't have to conform to the family standard or his dad's expectations. He just needed permission to be himself.

In the coming years, Ethan participated in science camps, 4-H, and road races, because he outran his brothers when they played outside. A music teacher discovered he was a great actor. These activities became his passions in middle school and high school. Our children need permission to say no to *our* expectations so they can say yes to God's gifts and callings.

FOSTERING INDIVIDUALITY AND AUTONOMY | Have you pushed your kids into sports or activities because *you* wanted them to? If so, you're not the first parent to have done so. I saw it often as a teacher of high school seniors. By their senior year, a lot of kids pull back from what they've done in high school because they've learned what *they* want to do. Autonomy and independence kick in.

Or maybe you have pushed your wishes for your child's post–high school plans or career. Again, it happens—a lot. But our kids aren't born for us to reinvent ourselves or to live out our unrealized dreams.

Seeing your kids do what you did (or wanted to do) when you were their age is a natural desire. But it's also rooted in self. It's called living through your kids, and it's a trap of the enemy. Living through your kids steals your responsibility to position them for the path God has for them. God wants you to train up your children in the way *they* should go, not the way *you* want them to go.

So how do you foster your teen or young adult's autonomous and independent identity? How do you step back and help a child who is different from you?

The first step is removing *your* expectations for your child, no matter the age. This is especially important in the high school years when teens are trying to figure out their career interests. Decisions about college and career paths can be overwhelming for teens. They can feel pressured, either directly or indirectly, to follow the career path suggested by their parents. Taking the next step—communicating support for your child's endeavors, which are different from yours—is helpful for both him and you. Verbal affirmation of a child's interest releases him from trying to please you and sets him on God's unique path.

Another step in fostering individuality is releasing children to their God-given personality and interests outside of career, sports, or extracurricular activities. This can be challenging, especially when your child has a temperament, way of thinking, or different interests from yours. Such children can frustrate you because you don't understand them or connect with them. You naturally may be at odds with them because they're so different. The kids who are different from you are the ones to spend extra time with so you get to know them.

You also might have a compliant or quiet child who doesn't directly oppose your views or suggestions. It's important to step back and ask such children what they want to do with their activities or career goals. These kids easily become the lost children in busy families.

These differences between you and your kids don't stop with sports, college choices, or career paths. The struggle between parent and child over autonomy, independence, and differences is a common area of conflict. If it's not handled well, relationships can be harmed, as can emotional and mental health. Kids protect themselves when their personhood is attacked. Most often, teens use negative coping mechanisms and other destructive behaviors when they don't feel safe being who they are.

It's exhausting trying to be someone you're not. Fight or flight causes some to want to give up.

Have you ever heard your teens or young adults say, "You don't have a clue" or "I don't care"? These types of statements are cues they don't think you understand them or what's going on in their life. It's more of a "need" statement than rebellion toward you or your position.

Your kids want you to accept them and be proud of them for *who they are* rather than for what they do. Focus on their strengths. Encourage their passions.

Don't be discouraged if you've put pressure or expectations on your kids. Most parents do at some point in time. No matter the age of your kids, embrace and support them where they currently are. If you have teens or young adults who you've put expectations on or who you haven't fully accepted, talk to them about it. Ask them for forgiveness. Then ask what they need from you to help change it.

THE YES PRINCIPLE | When your teens and young adults are exploring activities, ideas, or career interests, create safe environments for them to try new things while you still have guidance and input. Say yes to them in these scenarios as much as possible. Preteens and teens don't fully know their strengths and interests. Some are fighting to survive socially or emotionally and don't have time or energy to explore their gifts. The Psalm 127 model tells you to position your kids in the direction of their passion.

Autonomy and independence grow best when both successes and failures happen in a caring environment. Processing failure and mistakes while kids are still at home builds their confidence. Insecurity, on the other hand, can destroy strengths and passion.

However, saying yes and fostering your children's gifts can stretch you. You may be tempted to restrict your child's creativity or innovation because of fears, uncertainty, or impracticality. You may want to say no because a new activity takes up too much of your time. But the more experiences kids have, the more they learn what they *don't* want to do in addition to what they *do* want to do. They learn what ignites their passions.

Some activities may cost family time. When Jenna was a junior in high school, she asked to go on a mission trip to Mexico over Christmas vacation. I wanted to say no because we only had two Christmases left with her before she went to college. The practical side of me wanted to say, "You can do another trip later—one that's not over Christmas!"

But how do you say no to a teen's passion for mission work?

Jenna went on that trip and spent Christmas Day in an orphanage. She came back with a passion for orphan care. This trip clarified her college search and eventually took her to work with orphans in Guatemala, Haiti, and Mexico.

Had we said no because of the Christmas holiday, our daughter might have missed a life-defining opportunity. Letting your children spread their wings means taking your hands off and saying yes to God's direction, not yours.

God has a plan for our kids we can never imagine. We hold them loosely so they seek him as they discern the experiences he places in their lives.

In addition to helping your kids find their intrinsic passions, your teens and young adults also need opportunities that spark their career interests. Talk with them about their various classes in school. Support them in new activities they want to try.

Drew took a business foundations class his freshman year in high school and discovered he liked business. We are a family of people-helpers, not businesspeople. This class sparked an interest I never would have considered for him. We connected him with different business professionals in the community, and he finally got excited about college.

Intentional discussions about interests, likes, dislikes, hopes, and dreams make a clearer path for what's next after high school. The job options today are exponentially greater than they used to be thanks to technology and a global economy. Many careers that will be available in your child's lifetime aren't even invented yet! Giving your student access to various experiences helps her understand what she may or may not want to do for her career.

If your high school offers apprenticeship opportunities, vocational career classes, or specialized classes such as engineering, art, psychology, or business, encourage your teen to take these courses in addition to traditional classes. Visit colleges early so your children have a knowledge of potential majors and universities that might be right for them. We start college searches in the junior year so our teen can visit a college for a second time to narrow down choices.

Follow your child's lead for the college that fits him—small and private, large and public, commuting or online. Walk through the financial options together, but let the decision be his. If a child is unsure about college, don't rush him. Higher education is not for everyone. It's a big investment. It's okay if he doesn't go to college right after high school, or at all. Affirming your young adults' choices about vocation, education, and post–high school plans are important elements of letting them go.

Let your children figure it out, even if it takes a while. It's all part of growing up.

LETTING GO | Differentiating hopes, dreams, and expectations between you and your child is only one part of her being autonomous from you. The other component is separating emotionally from your child.

As your child gets older, it's tempting to hold her closer, to get *more* involved in her life than you were before. You may want to know what's going on in your teen's relationships not out of concern but because separation feels uncomfortable. There's a fine line between appropriate emotional attachment and unhealthy enmeshment between parent and child.

To navigate this area, ask yourself the following questions:

- Do you see your teen or young adult as your confidant?
- Does the thought of not taking care of your teen or young adult leave you despondent?

- Do you feel rejected or sad when your teen spends time with friends instead of you?
- Do you rely on your teen or young adult to meet your emotional needs? Do you seek your child's friendship first before you seek out your spouse or friends your age?
- Do you get angry or upset when your teen isn't friends with who you think he should be friends with?

If your answer is yes to one or more of these questions, step back and be wary of becoming enmeshed. Enmeshment happens when you're overinvolved with or overly concerned about your child's life; when you're jealous of her friendships; when you want control in her life; or when you rely on the relationship for how it makes *you* feel. Enmeshment subverts healthy autonomy for both parent and child. Enmeshment is harmful because your kids don't learn the boundary between you and them. They don't form their own thoughts and feelings because they focus on pleasing you. They do what you want, mimic your personality, and embrace your likes and dislikes until their identity is entwined with yours. In turn, an enmeshed parent smothers a child—speaks for her, takes care of her, and gets upset when she deviates from what the parent thinks she should do.

If you find yourself wondering if you've become enmeshed with your teen or young adult, keep asking questions. In the next chapters we'll cover how to give up control and allow your kids to struggle while also setting boundaries. These three concepts are intertwined, yet all are unique elements of building a healthy balance of autonomy, guidance, and release.

Your young adult is not a mini-you. Letting go is hard, and it starts with relinquishing control.

BUILDING UP
and letting go

Father, thank you for creating each of us as unique individuals. Thank you for the gifts you've created in me and the gifts you've given my children. Equip me to foster each child's strengths and passions. Help me to step back when I try to take over, and give me clarity if I am holding on too much. Amen.

1. Which of your children is most like you? Which one is most different from you?

2. Which child do you struggle with letting go of the most and why?

3. How can you help each of your children find their strengths or career path or passions?

4. Did you answer yes to any of the questions about enmeshment? Be honest with yourself about areas in which you need to separate from your child. What did you learn that can help you?

10

Give Up Control

Unless the Lord watches over the city, the guards stand watch in vain.
—PSALM 127:1

For Jenna, it was an overnight birthday party with the popular girls. For Mark, it was a sleepover with his teammates. For Drew, it was church camp when his older brother wouldn't be there. For Ethan, it was camping with his classroom buddy.

In each of these cases, Ron and I released the reins of control at appropriate ages, saying yes to these overnights even though we didn't feel completely comfortable. Our children were old enough we couldn't supervise them every waking moment. Each of these events was a leap of faith for this mama. That leap of faith continues every time I say yes when I'd rather keep my kids under my wings. My security in these moments is knowing Jesus is with my children when I can't be.

Have you had similar moments when you lie in bed wondering, What if he is exposed to something that will damage him forever? What if she is bullied or kids leave him out?

As your kids get older, the "what ifs" get louder: What if he takes drugs? What if she is assaulted? What if he gets hurt? What if they make the wrong decision or do something stupid? What if I'm not there when they need me?

These questions linger even with adult children. They roll around in your mind, driving worry, insecurity, and the need to control.

Giving up control isn't easy. Since the moment your baby was laid in your arms, you were in control. You decided what was best for her. You responded when she cried. You determined what she ate, what she wore, and where she went.

Slowly, though, she started doing things on her own, and you couldn't make every decision. She let you know she has a will of her own, with likes and dislikes. You've gradually let her make her own decisions. Now you have to let go of bigger things, like letting her live her own life.

The struggle for control never goes away. But you've never really been in control; God has been in control all along.

Do you trust God with your child's life? This is probably the most important question to ask yourself as a parent. Your answer will determine how you parent, how you release each child, and how you relate to your adult children.

Will you be a "my way" or "God's way" parent? Will you be a legalistic or relational parent? Will you be a fearful or faithful parent?

Let me challenge you with this question: If you can trust God with *your* life, can you trust him with the life of your child?

THE GREAT PROTECTOR | Psalm 127:1 says, "Unless the Lord watches over the city, the guards stand watch in vain." In this passage, standing guard actually means stepping away from the illusion of control. This mirrors the parenting experience, doesn't it? We think we're in control, but our kids have been moving away from us from their first day of life. This process is problematic when we fail to let go at appropriate stages. We develop blind spots that hinder our child's growth.

How do you *really* let go?

If you're like me, you let God take over in the Jesus-take-the-wheel moments, when you have little or no control over a situation. But most parenting happens in daily moments when you make ordinary decisions regarding your child. Unfortunately, there are no clear-cut instructions for when to hold on and when to let go as they grow and change. Relinquishing control goes against your mama-bear instinct. It makes you feel helpless. It puts a tightness in your chest because you've hovered over and protected your kids for a long time.

You lurked around the corner when you dropped them off at daycare or preschool to make sure they were okay. You stood at the top of the stairway when your daughter and her date were alone in the basement.

Have you hovered? I have.

But we can't guard our kids forever. Eventually it's time to let go. We can't influence their decisions or choices the way we used to. Psalm 127:1 establishes God as the guardian of the our children, not us.

GOD GAVE UP HIS CONTROL | The best instruction manual for relinquishing control is written by God himself. Psalm 139 beautifully declares that God created and knows everything about our children. He knows when each of them sit and when they rise. He knows their thoughts from afar. He saw their unformed bodies, and he created their inmost beings. He has a perfectly designed roadmap for each of them, but he doesn't give us Google maps for how to get them there.

What he does give us is intelligence and instinct to raise our children. But human wisdom is in vain without Christ at the center. God put an innate hunger for himself inside each of us. When you seek God's wisdom regarding your kids, he provides counsel through his Holy Spirit. Because God knows our children better than we do, he will give us wisdom and perspective when we ask.

Seeking God's wisdom and perspective is an act of faith when we no longer make their decisions. It's easier said than done, especially in areas like relationships, boundaries, and morality. Clarity in these areas happens through prayer, reading Scripture, godly discernment, and trusting God.

When Jenna was deciding which college to attend, she was choosing between a university three hours away from home and another that was eleven hours away. As the deadline for enrollment approached, I wanted to tell her to accept the offer at the closer university.

But the Holy Spirit convicted me: "If I'm calling her to the mission field, being that far away from home is just a stepping stone. I'm working in her, you just don't see it. If you don't back off, you'll interfere." God's rebuke was loud and clear.

God convicted me that he, not I, knew what was best for her future. I could actually get *in the way* of God working. My daughter was her own person and God knew what was better for her than I did.

It was a humbling lesson. Engineering what you think is best for your child's life might be hindering her own walk with God.

STRIKING AN EQUILIBRIUM | None of us want to be a helicopter parent. A helicopter parent is one who hovers and controls too much of their teen or young adult's life, thus delaying adulthood. Helicopter parents are everywhere today. Another version of the helicopter parent is the "lawnmower parent," who intercepts perceived hardship or trouble before it gets to a child. They control the child's path so it's easy for her. Neither of these parenting styles is healthy for you or your child.

Too much parental control creates young adults who live like children. They lack problem-solving skills and initiative and live in a culture of blame. They don't have to be accountable when others make their decisions for them.

Controlling when you should let go is disobedience to God and disrespects a teen or young adult's capabilities, intelligence, and independence. It leads to rebellion or passive defiance, both of which are unhealthy. It dishonors the person your child is becoming. It stunts his confidence and ability to make decisions of his own.

The opposite of too much control is no control: a hands-off parenting approach during adolescence. This is the cowardly road of parenthood, because it makes you a friend or peer to your child rather than the parent. That, too, is disobedience to Christ. Our responsibility is to guide, set boundaries, and confront our teens or young adults about unhealthy or harmful areas. Confronting isn't fun. The no-control approach avoids conflict so that your teen doesn't get mad at you.

Has your teen ever told you, "Everyone's doing it," or "You're the only parent who . . ."? Does guilt drive you to loosen boundaries too early because you're afraid your teen won't fit in? Do you fear judgment from other parents if you set a boundary stricter than theirs? These are real fears, but they shouldn't be the reason to take your hands completely off your teen's life.

It's natural for teens and young adults to test boundaries. But they expect you to set them. They know the crazy world that's out there. They battle that storm every day. They still need guidance. They look big and strong, but they don't have everything together. They expect an appropriate amount of control to help them figure things out.

Striking the right balance of control is exhausting when you've got young adults, high schoolers, and perhaps younger kids. It's easier to control or be more lenient with all of them because it takes less energy and forethought. Your young adults need you to let go, while your younger kids still need guidance while also growing independent. Balancing all of this involves evaluation, reassessment, and understanding that the process is not cut and dried.

But you're a warrior. Persevere and seek wisdom from the Holy Spirit. Moral issues, relationships, work ethics, and faith are difficult to navigate. Control in these areas depends on age, the individual child, the child's behavior, and how it affects the family. If the choices of a young adult living at home negatively influence younger kids, boundaries are necessary. The same is true for teens who are toxic or who make choices that require a parent's intervention. (We'll talk more about this in upcoming chapters.)

HOW TO GIVE UP CONTROL | How do you discern when to release control for each teen and young adult? Here are a few principles to consider:

1. You are the guardian of your child's soul during the childrearing years. God cares about your child's physical health and safety, but he is more concerned about her character and heart. Deuteronomy 6:5-9 reveals God's desire and his first priority for his children:

    > Love the Lord your God with all your heart and with all your soul and with all your strength. These commandments that I give you today are to be on your hearts. Impress them on your children. Talk about them when you sit at home and when you walk along the road, when you lie down and when you get up. Tie them as symbols on your hands and bind them on your foreheads. Write them on the doorframes of your houses and on your gates.

    As Christian parents, our responsibility is to protect and position our children's hearts toward Christ first and foremost. Foster a climate in your home and a relationship with your kids that cultivates hearts that will love God. Use relationship parenting rather than performance parenting. When you develop fertile ground in your children's souls, God's Word will grow when planted (Luke 8:1-15).

    Guarding your children's hearts also means setting appropriate boundaries for their physical, emotional, and spiritual well-being until they're adults. You may have to say no or "wait" to something that is harmful for their moral or emotional development. Peers may say, "They have to grow up some time," or "You can't shelter them forever." What you decide for your family may be different from what your peers decide. Each of us has to make our own decisions for our families according to our own belief system.

    As our children's guardians, we are accountable to God for what we've knowingly allowed into our child's lives. That is a sobering responsibility.

2. You actually give control to God. Giving up control has three action steps:
   - Release control in appropriate areas.
   - Trust your teen or young adult's ability to make decisions, regardless of whether you think these decisions are good or bad.
   - Trust that God has control and will work in your child's life.

   Ask for God's wisdom and perspective for releasing control in areas with each child. Tighter control for one child may be needed for discipline or safety or because of her maturity level. God will show you. Pray, seek God's counsel through his Word, and obey.

3. Lead and guide. Psalm 23:1-3 says, "The Lord is my shepherd, I lack nothing. He makes me lie down in green pastures, he leads me beside quiet waters, he refreshes my soul. He guides me along the right paths for his name's sake." According to these verses, God does three things before giving up control:
   - He *makes* us rest in his goodness.
   - He *leads* us in places of security.
   - He *refreshes* and prepares our soul for the work he has ahead of us.

   Then God steps aside and *guides*. A good leader knows when it's time to step aside and let those under her care take over. A good leader builds the skills and talents of subordinates so they are equipped to lead in their own time. A leader builds confidence in them. Then she lets others take over.

   God steps aside to guide us along right paths when we've learned to follow him. The same is true for our kids. Even if you don't think they can make decisions according to your standards, there's a time to step aside when your kids are of age. The transfer of power really goes from you back to the Father.

   It's his turn now to lead and guide your child's life. And your job is to follow him.

BUILDING UP
and letting go

Lord, thank you for being in control of my children's lives, whether I acknowledge it or not. Give me your wisdom for when to hold on and when to let go. Thank you for reminding me I can trust you with my kids. Amen.

1. What are your "what if" fears regarding giving up control?

2. In what parenting area is God prompting you to give up control? In what ways do you believe God will provide?

3. Do you struggle more with being a helicopter parent or a disengaged parent? If so, what changes can you make to be more balanced?

4. What is one principle you can apply to your family right now?

11

Don't Steal the Struggle

My God will meet all your needs according to the riches of his glory in Christ Jesus.
—PHILIPPIANS 4:19

"How is he doing?" several people asked me during Mark's junior season of varsity basketball. Basketball is king in our little Hoosier town, where the Saturday morning coffee shop talk is about last night's game, what the coach is doing wrong, and how things aren't fair for the hometown boys.

It was a hard season for Mark because he didn't get much playing time. Mostly he sat on the bench, though he had been a starting player since middle school. People thought it was unfair and were quick to tell us. It was hard for his dad and me as we watched him work hard but still be told he needed to improve.

"You need to be quicker, and you have to work harder," the coach told Mark, and Ron understood the coach's reasoning. Though Mark's natural talents carried him in junior high and junior varsity, at the varsity level he needed to be quicker. If he wanted to play, he had to do the work.

Personally, I wanted to steal the struggle from him. It was tempting to complain, to join in the rant about unfairness that people threw our way, or to suggest to Mark that he quit. But while I wanted to say how unfair the situation was, Mark didn't give me the chance. He never complained about sitting on the bench, and he never badmouthed the coach to us. I learned my son could take harsh criticism, face disappointment, and persevere through a struggle that changed him for the better.

The following year, Mark was a starter, and he became a leader for the team. He was an example to his younger brothers for how to take criticism and work for what you want.

I learned a lot that year. Maybe even more than Mark did.

Have you ever wanted to rescue your kid?

Most of us do. But stealing the struggle from your kids isn't the answer. Equipping them for life's challenges is.

LIVING IN AN AGE OF ENTITLEMENT | "Suffering produces perseverance; perseverance, character; and character, hope" says Romans 5:3-4. Suffering, however, is not part of the cultural paradigm in which your teen or young adult lives. Whether you like it or not, your children are part of the "entitlement generation." They're influenced by technology, social media, music, education, peers, and friends. How do you equip your kids to be responsible adults in a culture of selfies, instant gratification, and participation trophies?

We've already covered the first steps for developing autonomy and giving up control. Allowing your kids to struggle is the next step in preparing them to successfully fledge the nest.

Overcoming challenges, problem solving, and persevering are critical life skills that are almost becoming extinct. Teaching these skills is an important job because real life is full of adversity and pain.

It's uncomfortable to watch your teens and young adults struggle. You want to swoop in, fix things, and make sure they're happy. Revisit that vision you cast for your family in earlier chapters. Are the goals centered around responsibility or happiness? If you just want your kids to be happy, you're a candidate for becoming a helicopter parent who enables and entitles. It's a subtle trap in which parents can easily get caught.

Examine your perspective about entitlement. Do you rescue because you don't want to see your kids hurt? Do you try to make them happy even though they're old enough to face consequences?

Temporary pain builds a stronger threshold for greater trials. Rescuing your children, however, subverts their confidence. Mark's basketball experience was a minimal example of persevering through trial. But his confidence and determination grew through the experience. Harder things have come to our kids' lives since then. Your kids will have hard things too.

God doesn't spare us from suffering. Romans 5 says suffering produces perseverance, perseverance produces character, and character produces hope. Hope and strength come from Christ himself. Philippians 4:19 says that God will supply all your needs according to God's glorious riches in Christ Jesus. In the most difficult circumstances, God meets your needs in unimaginable ways.

Rescuing your child isn't your job. Allowing God to work in your child's life is.

Your kids may test your limits when you don't rescue. They may make you feel guilty. Don't give in to false guilt. When you love and support them through their struggles, they know your love is unconditional.

Kids need adversity to grow and mature. When *you* fill these needs, you steal opportunities for them to grow and experience God's power and comfort in their life.

That's not twisted theology. It's life. Being an adult means you figure things out on your own. Consider the world of entitlement your children live in. Equipping your young adults with problem-solving skills, perseverance, and the ability to work hard will make them remarkable leaders in their culture. Their resilience will provide hope and strength to others.

They will be leaders whether they plan to be or not. God may even use their strength from a struggle "for such a time as this" (Esther 4:14).

I DON'T WANT TO ADULT TODAY! | Have you heard the phrase "I don't want to adult today"? It's a common expression among young adults. It means "I don't want to be or act like an adult today." It may refer to simple responsibilities such as getting a car serviced or paying bills, or to behavior such as dealing with emotions or the day's events in a responsible manner.

Being an adult has become a verb. Acting like one is now a choice.

Unfortunately, life doesn't ask you if you feel like "adulting." Entitlement feeds this Peter Pan syndrome, and so does enabling. Enabling occurs when a person facilitates or supports someone else's unhealthy behavior. Though it is often a well-meaning attempt to offer care and support, enabling keeps kids and adults trapped in immature, irresponsible, and often destructive behavior. It prevents a person from growing, persevering, and changing. Enabling shelters a teen or young adult from the consequences of irresponsible, inappropriate, or destructive choices.

Enabling easily creeps into parent-child relationships, making you feel like you're helping your child when you are actually hurting her instead.

Parents enable when they support or excuse unhealthy behavior. Rescuing others can actually become a coping mechanism for the enabler. Enablers don't like facing conflict, feeling pain, disappointing others, or having people upset with them. They please people, including their child, at the expense of their health and the health of others. They avoid saying no because they don't want their children to be mad at them.

False guilt and insecurities also motivate enabling. You believe you're a good parent if you let your children do what they want or what makes them happy. Enabling feeds the dream that life is good when everyone's happy. It's one of the most destructive lies there is. We've created a culture in which happiness is the ultimate goal and feeling bad is avoided at all costs.

Social media has enabled this culture by being a source of instant happiness and good feelings. You post a picture and fixate on the number of likes or hits it receives. According to one report, the average teen checks social media one hundred times a day, mainly in search of affirmation.[1] The quest for affirmation is connected to dopamine, the feel-good hormone that is activated, for one, through the anticipation of receiving positive comments or responses from social media and texts.[2] Teens are constantly searching for affirmation. Receiving a text means they're important and connected with others. Kids are wiring their brains to seek instant gratification at younger and younger ages; many children in elementary school are texting, are on social media, and even have their own YouTube channels.

All of this is causing teens and young adults to lack healthy coping skills for even the smallest threshold of pain. Kids are escaping from pain through prescription drug abuse, street drugs, alcohol, cutting, and other self-harming behaviors. Depression, anxiety, and suicidal ideation is increasing.

Self-control and perseverance are still necessary skills for teens to cope with pain. Pain is God's natural warning that something isn't right. It prompts problem solving and strength. When your child knows strength and resilience from pushing through pain, she will become a source of hope among her peers.

God doesn't shield us from pain; he is with us in it. God also never abandons or ignores our cries for help. Throughout Scripture, God meets people's needs for their good and his glory. He prioritizes *joy* over *happiness*, *long term* over *short term*. He allows pain to draw us to him. James writes, "Consider it pure joy, my brothers and sisters, whenever you face trials of many kinds, because you know that the testing of your faith produces perseverance. Let perseverance finish its work so that you may be mature and complete, not lacking anything" (James 1:2-4).

---

1. Chuck Hadad, "Why Some 13-Year-Olds Check Social Media 100 Times a Day," CNN.com, October 13, 2015, http://www.cnn.com/2015/10/05/health /being-13-teens-social-media-study/.
2. Susan Weinschenk, "Why We're All Addicted to Texts, Twitter and Google," *Psychology Today*, September 11, 2012, https://www.psychologytoday.com/blog /brain-wise/201209/why-were-all-addicted-texts-twitter-and-google.

WHOM THEY NEED THE MOST | For years, food numbed my pain. Food is what I ran to when I was hurt or angry. I persevered and overcame anorexia and bulimia so I could model healthy coping mechanisms for my kids. I had to practice self-control and commit to healthy, alternative ways to deal with pain. It's a gift I have given my family, though they may not even know it.

My relationship with God made the journey possible. In my darkest, most private moments, God was there. First Corinthians contains the truth that convicted and spurred me to be victorious over unhealthy behavior: "Everything is permissible, but not everything is beneficial" (1 Corinthians 10:23 CSB). It's permissible to circumvent or numb pain, but it's not beneficial.

Our kids watch how we respond to pain and adversity. When your kids see you appropriately handle pain through an authentic relationship with Christ, it gives them hope that's absent from their culture. I've tried to be honest with my kids about the painful areas of my life which are appropriate for them to know. Hiding pain doesn't allow your kids to witness God's work in your life, marriage, or family. Showing them how God meets your needs in adversity equips them to trust God when facing tough things on their own.

We are created to hunger and thirst for God. When we allow God to provide our needs—socially, emotionally, physically, and spiritually—we learn that no matter what happens in our lives, God's peace passes all understanding. God becomes personal to our kids when they see him meet the most intimate needs in our life and theirs.

How do you show your children practical faith and God's provision?

Instead of rescuing, share your stories of how God has helped you. Share how you apply Scripture to your life. One of my favorite passages for adversity is Joshua 1:7-9: "Be strong and very courageous. . . . Keep this Book of the Law always on your lips; meditate on it day and night, so that you may be careful to do everything written in it. Then you will be prosperous and successful. Have I not commanded you? Be strong and courageous. Do not be afraid;

do not be discouraged, for the Lord your God will be with you wherever you go." I pray this with my kids at the beginning of each school year. They need to hear these words out loud.

Peers, media, and culture won't tell your kids to be strong and courageous; these sources will tell them to be angry if they don't get what they want. How do you help them be strong?

- Make your kids be responsible for basic skills. Simple things like doing laundry, paying for car insurance and personal products, and getting a job are basic things kids should be doing on their own during the teen and college years.
- Support your child's teachers or coaches. Empathize when things aren't fair, but don't blame. When your college student fails a test, give him suggestions but don't rescue him. Let your child know he shouldn't receive special treatment (even when you secretly think he should). School situations are microcosms of the real world.
- As much as you can, equip your child to take care of problems at school, work, or socially on her own without you taking the reins. Kids are more resilient than you think. You rob your children of tapping into that resilience when you enable their quest for happiness and validation.

Kids *will* figure things out, one way or another. They learn the best when they know they've got what it takes to meet the challenge. They'll learn to adult because . . . they're adults.

THE EXCEPTIONS | Not all pain, however, should be left for kids or young adults to handle alone. Pain from any type of sexual, emotional, spiritual, or physical abuse is never something to be ignored, downplayed, or left for a teen or young adult to deal with by themselves. The same is true for suicidal ideation, self-harm, depression, or mental health conditions. A young person reporting these things should get professional help from counselors, mental health agencies, family doctors, or organizations specializing in these areas. Kids need appropriate, healthy coping skills to be strong and courageous. God uses the wisdom and compassion of professionals, mentors, and experts to meet these needs.

Second, if *you* have contributed to the pain or problem of your child, acknowledge it, ask for forgiveness, and change what needs to be changed. If necessary, seek professional help for yourself or for your family so you can be in a healthy place to help your teen or young adult. If you've created a codependent relationship or have been an enabler, diligently seek resources so you can break free from unhealthy patterns and build a healthy family.

Parents don't have to be perfect, but we do have to be responsible for our stuff and help our kids take care of theirs.

BUILDING UP
and letting go

Thank you, Father, for being the comforter and sustainer through all our struggles. Thank you for being with my kids through their struggles. Help me to trust you with the pain of my child's life. Convict me in areas in which I need to step back and let my kids grow through their struggle. Amen.

1. What is the hardest part for you in letting your kids experience pain or adversity?

2. Are there any areas in which you are enabling one (or more) of your kids? If so, what can you do to change that?

3. What is one principle you can apply to your family today?

12

Set Boundaries

You hem me in behind and before, and you lay your hand upon me. Such knowledge is too wonderful for me, too lofty for me to attain.
—PSALM 139:5-6

I had a pit in my stomach. I had come across music my teen was listening to that made me sick. The lyrics were sexually explicit, abusive, violent, and demeaning toward women. They were vile and appalling, especially because of my work as a counselor to women in abusive relationships. That evening I knew I had to confront my son when he came home from his sports practice. The simpler days of confronting younger children were long gone. Confronting teens who are taller and more adultlike is not on the most-desired activities list for moms.

But it was necessary. It was a boundary I needed to enforce. Music is a powerful influence in a teen's life, and this message was not acceptable in our home.

When my son came home, I told him the music didn't honor God and didn't respect women. I told him it had to go. I braced myself for his response. It all came, just as I expected: angry words, shouting, and the furious words "You're the only mom who does stuff like this!"

I wish I could say I was strong and took the confrontation with confidence and ease. But that would be lying.

After my son stormed off, I was sad and exhausted. I stood there, doubting myself. Just a few minutes before, I was certain I was doing the right thing. But now I wondered: Am I overreacting? Am I the only mom who cares about the music her son listens to? Don't I need to let him make these decisions on his own? Was it really that big of a deal?

Self-doubt is natural when setting boundaries with your teens and young adults, especially when those boundaries seem countercultural or old-fashioned. But our parental responsibility is to teach and model God's standards, even when the culture doesn't. Lyrics filled with hate, violence, and sexual assault had no place in the ears of a son while under my roof. I told him to remove the music from his device and find other music that was not offensive to God, me, or women. I explained how the words didn't represent what we believe as a family or as Christians. I told him the words were real to me because of women I care about.

Confronting kids isn't fun, especially when they're almost adults. But teens are not adults, and they still need boundaries. Enforcing them is challenging. Boundaries with your teens go over better when you share the moral reason why instead of saying "Because I said so." It's where relationship parenting versus performance parenting really pays off.

Over the next few days, offensive music disappeared and new music showed up on his iTunes account. I checked out the new artists and their lyrics. He found Christian rappers whose lyrics were God-honoring. The battle was worth the conflict to bring healthy music that would penetrate his mind. We saw his demeanor change during his senior year of high school as he became a fan of one particular Christian rap artist. He wrote essays in English class about how the music affected him. He, in turn, influenced his younger brothers. They even went to a concert together—three brothers, from high school to middle school, rapping to godly music.

I learned a lot the day I had that conversation with my son. I learned kids will push the boundaries you set, but that God works within those boundaries. I learned that God uses for good what the enemy wants to destroy (Genesis 50:20).

EMBRACING GOD'S BOUNDARIES | God is a God of boundaries, protection, wisdom, and guidance. He sets principles in Scripture for our physical, emotional, and moral health and safety. You can trust God's boundaries in all areas of life, using his principles with your teens and young adult children. Psalm 139:5 is a beautiful picture of God's protective boundaries: "You hem me in behind and before, and you lay your hand upon me."

God sets boundaries behind and before us. He hems us in. In simplest terms, a hem is made to prevent clothes from unraveling. I love the idea that God protects us from unraveling, don't you?

Boundaries start with our toddlers, when we say things like "Don't touch the stove; it's hot!" We physically protect our kids when they're young, adjusting the boundaries as they get older. But their mental, emotional, and spiritual well-being also needs protection. Somewhere between toddlerhood and the teenage years, parental authority and boundaries get blurred. Questions such as "How can I enforce it?" and arguments like "Everyone else is doing it" plague us.

So how do you know what boundaries to set, especially when you're supposed to be relinquishing control?

Technology is one area where you need to set boundaries. Pornography, predators, hate speech, harassment, sexting, and stalking are possibilities for your kids any time they are online. Music, movies, apps, and social media influence the belief systems and character development of teens and young adults more than we realize. Online predators are everywhere your kids are. Social media is the most prominent place where teens are groomed for sex trafficking and exploitation. I've known kids as young as ten to be approached by online predators inviting them into inappropriate relationships. Pictures and videos are sent back and forth between teens without adults ever knowing what's sent. Pornography use is increasing, and the perception of pornography is changing among teens and young adults. A majority of teens and young adults don't perceive porn as a problem. According to a 2016 study by the Barna Group, a Christian research firm, only 32 percent of youth ages thirteen to twenty-four said viewing porn was wrong. Eighteen- to twenty-four-year-olds are the most frequent viewers of porn, and 57 percent of young adults report seeking out porn either daily, weekly, or monthly.[1]

A conversation I had with a middle school student made me realize the broader acceptance and desensitization of porn: he thought porn was a normal part of teen sexuality, even in middle school.

You are a pioneer parent in the age of screen time, secret apps, chatrooms, and sexting. Remember your role as guardians of your children's souls? We are responsible to God for what we knowingly let into the minds and hearts of our sons and daughters. We have to be vigilant and engaged where our kids are.

It's hard. It's scary. But it's critical.

In areas of morality, emotional health, and physical safety, appropriate boundaries still are part of the parenting job with underage kids.

The principle from 1 Corinthians 10:23 is a guiding principle for boundary setting: "Everything is permissible, but not everything is beneficial" (CSB). Your children have access to and can do anything, really, that they please. But it doesn't mean it's healthy.

Does that alarm you? It should. You have two choices: you can disengage, because it seems futile to keep up, or you can set appropriate boundaries for the age of each child. Draw close to God when setting boundaries, seeking his counsel for each child. What one child needs in terms of boundaries may be different from what a sibling needs. The more you trust God with the boundaries, the less anxious and insecure you will be of the outcome when kids challenge you or peers question you.

---

1. Barna Research Group, "Porn in the Digital Age: New Research Reveals 10 Trends," April 6, 2016, https://www.barna.com/research/porn-in-the-digital-age-new-research-reveals-10-trends/.

Our family technology policy includes several principles, beginning in early adolescence. We are engaged on the social media platforms of the teen in the house so one of us knows how they function, both positively and negatively. We use a parent-control technology filter on devices and phones, have passwords to our teens' devices, and have an open-door policy to check their apps as long as they're in high school. These safeguards take time, research, and active engagement. I often hear parents say they can't keep up with all the technology or that their kids don't want them to be where they are on social media. But we wouldn't put our kids in a car without safety features or send them to drive on a dangerous freeway without any training. We also just wouldn't let them hang out with just anyone in real life without checking things out first. As with all other situations that have the potential for physical, emotional, or spiritual harm, we as parents have to equip our kids to be as safe as possible in potentially dangerous situations.

Your technology guidelines may be different. Each of us needs to seek God's wisdom for what's best for our kids and family.

If you're afraid your teen will be left out or ridiculed because of your boundaries, stand firm and have hope that God cares about these areas, too. Parenting out of fear creates unhealthy boundaries: you either build walls out of fear or don't enforce boundaries because you're afraid they will suffer if you're too strict. Neither one of these extremes is healthy.

Protective boundaries *will* be challenged, but kids want them. Really.

REASSESSING BOUNDARIES | During the writing of this book, we reassessed our technology boundaries. Rules that had applied to the older kids were not relevant for Ethan, our youngest, whose teen culture was different from his that of his siblings, even those just a couple of years older. As technology and culture change, boundaries may change as a result. However, the principles behind the boundaries should stay the same.

Ethan was happy with the new freedoms we gave him, but still questioned the restrictions. I shared with him the biblical principles for our boundaries, along with what I learned from his older siblings' experiences. A few years earlier, I asked one of the older boys if we should have been more lenient on unlimited Wi-Fi access at younger ages. He said, "No, Mom, it was probably a good thing."

That taught me a lot, coming from an older teen who knew what went on among his peers and was aware of his own struggles.

I shared this response with Ethan, along with some experiences I've had working with youth. In the end, he respected the boundaries we set.

According to Romans 14:12, when you and I meet God face-to-face, we'll have to give an account for the boundaries, or lack thereof, for each of our children. I won't be accountable for your kids, and you won't be accountable for mine. We'll be asked if we were faithful in impressing God's ways on the hearts of our children. Deuteronomy 6 calls us to set boundaries not only for their protection but because we love God with our heart, soul, and mind and strength.

When you and I love God above all else, we will protect our children in his ways so that they, too, will learn about his love, care, and protection. We will value this over peer pressure, the culture, what's politically correct, or the current fads and trends. We will love our children rather than sell their souls to be popular. We will be the guardians of their souls for the appropriate time God has given us to raise them before they go into the storms of life.

When they learn the goodness of God's boundaries, they will know the peace, safety, and security that lies within them.

BOUNDARIES AND TOUGH LOVE | If boundaries about music and cell phones were the only ones we needed to enforce, parenting wouldn't be so bad. With teens and young adults, there will likely be bigger challenges. Christians are not immune from complications of mental health issues, toxic relationships, abuse, sexual promiscuity, addiction, or other harmful behaviors that affect a family. A common scenario is a teen or young adult who lives at home and disrespects siblings or parents, or whose toxic behavior affects the family or younger siblings. This can even be true for underage teens whose toxic or destructive behavior affects younger siblings or the entire family.

Setting boundaries with toxic or destructive kids requires tough love—making decisions for their treatment or setting boundaries for their health and safety and that of the family. For minors, getting professional treatment for the problem *is* within your realm of responsibility. A teenager may challenge it, but you are still her guardian, and it's essential for her to get help when she is still a minor.

When teens are over eighteen or have graduated from high school, it's harder to get them help if they're not willing. However, keeping them in the home when their toxic behavior is harming the family is a sign of enabling. One of the hardest things a parent does with a toxic young adult is to require him to move out or to call the authorities when his destructive behavior is hurting the health and safety of the family. It's also one of the most necessary interventions if he is to get long-term help or face his problems. Rock-bottom pain is some of the worst pain, but it also can bring about a desire to change and get help.

You're not a bad parent when you practice tough love. Shutting the door on your hurting, toxic child or telling her she can't come home is one of the hardest things you may ever do.

But God is with such children, and God is with you. He is the Lord of your family, and your story isn't done.

The same is true for abusive or crisis situations. Your teen or young adult may be the victim of a dating relationship that's toxic or abusive, or may have mental health conditions that make him a danger to himself or others. There's a time for parents to step in for the health and safety of their kids, no matter what. There are professional resources for almost every situation. Setting boundaries in these areas may take time and money, but these situations are worth the fight.

Remember the house that stands firm through the storm? That house has a strong foundation, tough walls, and a strong structure built for protection. That's what you build when you stand firm in Christ in the battles that may destroy those you love.

You are not fighting alone. Jesus is on the front line of the battle when you let him lead. He hems you in—behind and before. He is your hope in the storm and your joy in the morning.

BUILDING UP
and letting go

Father, thank you for setting boundaries in our lives. Thank you for being my strength and wisdom for the boundaries I need to set for each of my kids. Equip me to know which boundaries to set and which battles to fight. Thank you for sufficiently providing in every way in the life of my family. Amen.

1. What fears do you have about setting boundaries for your kids?

2. Are there boundaries you need to readjust? To strengthen or loosen?

3. What comfort or strength do you get when you remember that Christ sets boundaries around your family and that he's fighting battles with you?

4. What's one principle you can apply to your situation right now?

13

Beyond the Picture-Perfect Image

He will wipe every tear from their eyes. There will be no more death or mourning or crying or pain, for the old order of things has passed away.
—REVELATION 21:4

"How is Tony's year going?" I asked Rachel as we sat on the bleachers watching our kids at a sporting event.

Rachel hesitated and then said, "It's been better." I asked a few questions, and then she unloaded. Things were not okay at home. Tony was out of control and his behavior was affecting his younger siblings.

It's a familiar story line in Christian homes. Somewhere between the full house and empty nest, there's pain. A young adult with an unplanned pregnancy. A teen with an addiction. The spouse who no longer wants to be married. The college student who rejects the morals and faith in which she was raised.

These scenarios happen in real families. These parents are my friends and yours.

They are me and you.

We are the families living beyond the picture-perfect image. You may be living a life you didn't think you'd be living, the one you hide with busyness, activities, and sugar-coated answers.

I understood Rachel's hesitation to answer a simple question. Pain understands pain. From the years of our own family's struggles, I was familiar with assessing who was safe to talk to and who wasn't. You don't just dump your mess out there for everyone to see. That's too risky. You're afraid to be judged. So you put on your happy face and pretend things are okay because you think you're the only one whose family is a mess. Everyone else looks all put together in the bleachers, on Instagram, and in the church pew.

But they're not. Most of us have a story that's not picture perfect. We need to be more real with each other.

Walking the path of brokenness myself and with others has taught me that Christians need safe places to share their struggles. Through writing my Life Beyond the Picket Fence blog, sharing my testimony, and counseling clients, I've learned that almost everyone has a story of brokenness. Many of us struggling are those with kids both in and out of home. We're stressed and exhausted by trying to keep things together, and we desperately need a safe place to land without judgment, condemnation, or shame.

We need hope. We need each other. We need to know how to navigate the harsh realities we may encounter with our kids. And we need to change our expectations and dispel the myth of the picture-perfect family.

REDEFINING EXPECTATIONS | Being real with one another starts with setting realistic expectations. There's a false belief held by many Christians that if you do things the right way, you'll live happily ever after. But that only happens in storybook endings. Pain and hardship are part of this earthly life. Only when we are in the presence of Jesus Christ in heaven will there be no more death, mourning, crying, or pain, because the old order of things will have passed away (Revelation 21:4).

You and I live in the old order—between the garden of Eden and the glory of Christ's presence. There's hardship and sin in this earthly life. Yet many of us expect that we are guaranteed to have a happy Christian family if we profess faith in Jesus Christ and do what's right.

At least that's what I believed. So when mess instead of bliss is your reality, you hide behind the image. You smile, deflect questions, and keep conversations short and cordial. You feel vulnerable and fear judgment. If people *really* knew what was going on at your house, they might reject you.

I want you to know you are not alone if your family is struggling with the things we've been talking about. Experience has taught me that young adults and teens usually struggle with *something*. That struggle often happens before your nest is empty, and it's why we've spent several chapters talking about these battles with kids. Dealing with a child's problems is exhausting, especially when you have younger kids at home. It's the stuff you don't post on social media. You don't snap a picture of the fight you just had or write about the disturbing phone call you just got.

Being a Christian doesn't exclude your kids from messing up. But your child's problems don't define you as a parent. Redefining expectations is necessary so families can support one another with grace and compassion in safe places. Painful things can devastate you, especially if you think bad things won't happen to you or your kids. We need to give grace to one another when adversity hits.

Your children's struggles can also paralyze you if you let them define your faith, your family, or your parenting. It's not accurate to define yourself by the choices your kids make. That's performance parenting. The most well-intentioned parents still have kids who make poor decisions or walk away from the faith. Your identity is separate from your role as parent.

Childrearing isn't about raising perfect kids; it's about positioning your children toward God and equipping them to "adult" well. Prayer and relationship are the means by which you support and guide them for the decades after.

The following are truths about parenting that help us redefine our expectations and equip us for some of the most difficult parenting experiences:

- Your children are separate from you, and their choices are their own.
- Your children's decisions don't define you.
- Your children's decisions don't define them.
- Children's choices are for a moment in time. They can change, and so can the outcome of their story.
- Your relationship with your children is more important than their decisions or lifestyles.
- You can set boundaries and still have a positive relationship with your children.
- People who judge are not the ones with whom you should concern yourself.
- A rogue child does not have to destroy your family.
- God heals and restores relationships and people.
- There's freedom when you're honest with yourself.
- Your kids will mess up because they're not perfect, and neither are you.
- Love your family for who they are, not for their performance or how people perceive them.
- Parents need safe places with other parents.
- God is the hope for all families.

Which truths do you need to apply to your family?

FOCUS ON YOUR FAMILY | A phrase I often hear from others is "What will people think?" This is not a good principle by which to guide your family. Parenting for the sake of appearances won't get you through the hard stuff we've been talking about. If there's adversity in your home or marriage, focus on health and healing rather than on your image.

So where do you seek hope and healing? Where do you run when things are a mess? The first place to run is to God. People will fail you, but God never will.

I ran to God when we needed hope and healing. He was safe. Our mess, however, was a result of my poor choices rather than the choices of others. But God saw my sin and forgave me. He loved my teens when I didn't love well. He saw the tears. God was with our family, standing in grace, forgiveness, and truth. I realized I could be completely honest with God. He was faithful. He heard and answered our prayers.

Though God is the healer of all things, healing often doesn't begin until we pursue healing through personal responsibility or, in many cases, professional help. I had to honestly look at what wasn't working in our family life. I had to deal with my anger and stress. With only a few years before Jenna left for college, my expectations and priorities shifted. I stopped striving to *do* what I thought I should be doing and focused on what was best for our family. Though Ron was supportive and helped with each aspect of family life, I had to look at my own stress levels and how it was affecting our family. I changed careers, stepped back from other responsibilities, practiced self-care, and focused on this season of my family's life. I needed to be engaged in and available at home instead of volunteering for every school and church event just for the sake of appearances. When I stepped away from leadership in several areas, others stepped in and contributed. I needed to take care of my issues so I could parent better in the remaining years of childrearing.

I'm still doing that. It was a lifestyle change. Busyness doesn't go away as your kids leave the house. You can replace every hour you spent at a high school event with some other "good" activity that drains you or keeps you from being mentally, emotionally, or spiritually healthy.

Parents' issues affect kids. Misplaced priorities affect kids. There's a balance between parental blame and parental responsibility. A parent can't be blamed for all the choices a teen or young adult makes. Yet we *are* responsible when our hurts, unhealthy habits, and unresolved issues prevent us from parenting well. Our kids need healthy parents to guide them through the storms of adolescence and early adulthood.

Your role as a childrearer is limited to only a few short years. Kids in mid-to-late adolescence still need our emotional availability, engagement, and guidance, because teens and young adults have more problems than in past generations. A 2016 *Time* cover story featured the epidemic of kids struggling with depression, anxiety, self-harm, and suicidal ideation.[1] According to the National Alliance on Mental Illness, one in five kids from the ages of thirteen to eighteen live with a mental health condition.[2] Their generation is the first to deal with the new phenomena of technology, social media, instant communication, and access to anyone, anywhere, with anything. There's more isolation from face-to-face relationships because of it.

Your kids need you. When you and I are too busy, or dealing with our own emotional messes, or simply not making ourselves available to them, we're missing what they need. Christian parents can have unrealistic expectations of what kids face in their middle school, high school, and college or post–high school experiences. Parents often assume that if their kids are hanging out with good peers or are enrolled at a good school, they won't be exposed to certain things. With the rise of cultural violence, hypersexuality, and the demands of social media, teens today face different challenges than prior generations did. Your child needs you to be approachable, available, and to take their hurt seriously.

When your kids share something they're struggling with, don't look shocked. Just listen. Be approachable and compassionate. Talk with them about their needs. If professional resources are needed, don't hesitate to get services. And don't worry about what people will think.

No one else is going to fight for the health of your child or your family. You're parenting in a disconnected and hurting culture. Your child and your child's generation need you.

I was once told by a high school student I taught that I live in a fairytale world because I appeared to have it all together—the perfect house, the perfect family, the perfect life. Every day he drove by my house with its front porch and white picket fence.

---

1. Susanna Shrobsdorff, "Teen Depression and Anxiety: Why the Kids Are Not Alright," *Time*, October 27, 2016, http://time.com/4547322/american-teens-anxious-depressed-overwhelmed/.
2. National Alliance on Mental Illness, "Mental Health Facts: Children and Teens," accessed August 24, 2017, https://www.nami.org/getattachment/Learn-More/Mental-Health-by-the-Numbers/childrenmhfacts.pdf.

It was different from his world just a few miles away, where his mom, a single parent, worked hard just to pay the rent. It was a life-altering conversation. I realized how damaging the veneer of a picture-perfect image is to the testimony of Christ in a hurting world. In this generation of mourning, death, crying, and pain, we have the greatest opportunity to give witness to an authentic faith—to our kids and everyone else who is watching.

Our culture needs authentic families to testify that God is evident in the midst of adversity, pain, or sin. Other families need to see you being real so that they can feel safe with their messes. In an authentic community of faith, God is glorified and others are given hope.

THE BIG DISAPPOINTMENT | Living authentically also means being real about disappointment with your child's actions, attitudes, apathy, or choices. Disappointment is hard to face because doubts, prejudices, and pride rise to the surface. The unwritten rule of parenting is that our kids reflect our parenting and our values. When they succeed and excel, we pat ourselves on the back for doing a great job. When they disappoint, we often feel shame and perceive contempt from others. We're embarrassed at our children's choices, lifestyle, or behavior.

Doubt and insecurity creep in. We wonder what we did wrong.

No matter the disappointing circumstances, it's important to get past your disappointment so you can maintain a healthy relationship with your child. Remember: relationship parenting is more important than performance parenting. There's a difference between being disappointed in your child's actions and being disappointed in who he is as a person. The latter is damaging. In the parable of the prodigal son (Luke 15:11-32), the father was disappointed by the choices his son made, but he did not dwell on his son's failures. He embraced and loved the child for who he was and because he was his son.

In the recesses of their souls, kids don't want to disappoint us. They long to see pride and joy in our eyes. Beginning in early childhood, though, they learn when we are disappointed. They see it on our faces. However, in their quest for independence, they're challenged between pleasing us or finding what makes them happy. They engage in a myriad of experiences that teach them, in both healthy and unhealthy ways, what they want in life. Some of these choices can devastate us.

Our kids *will* disappoint us. What you and I do with this disappointment is the question.

Your teen, young adult, or adult child still needs to know you love her even when her behavior or life choices disappoint you. Your relationship with her is for a lifetime, and she still looks to your face to see that unconditional love she longs for.

Another aspect of disappointment, though, is our doing. Too often we parents set high expectations that our kids can't or don't want to meet. It's sobering to acknowledge that these pressures and expectations are *our* issue, not our child's. These disappointments stem from topics we've already mentioned regarding control, living through our children, and enmeshed identities.

We need to let go of *our* idea of who our children should be and pursue an authentic relationship with them that models Christ.

THE ESTRANGED CHILD | Sarah's younger son was friends with one of mine. She and I were chatting one day when I asked about her older kids, who were out of college. Sarah told me, through tears, that they hadn't talked to one of their kids in more than a year. Sarah's daughter had a different lifestyle than what she was raised with. When her parents tried to contact her, she would blow them off, and finally she told them to get out of her life. She changed her phone number and hadn't been home in over a year. Sarah was devastated.

The estranged relationship affected the younger siblings at home. Holidays without their sister were hard. Sarah's husband was diagnosed with a medical condition during the time, and their daughter still didn't come around.

Parent pain is deep pain.

Jessica was a friend of mine from college. Her oldest son was a college student living at home who was in and out of rehab for alcohol and drug abuse. He continued to drink and do drugs at home while their youngest was still in high school. Jessica and her husband called the cops several times, and the court system eventually forced him to get treatment. At first her son was angry and bitter that his parents turned him in for violating probation. He didn't speak to them for several months. Finally, in the court-ordered rehab center, her son decided to overcome his addiction. Within two years, he was clean from drugs, restored to his family, and excited about his new love for Christ.

Just a few years earlier, these women had been busy with sports schedules, music concerts, and the revolving door we've been talking about. They never anticipated the paths their children would take, or that they would be estranged from their kids for long periods of time.

Each of them are godly women who love Christ and who are raising their families with solid Christian values. Their stories offer real examples of parents doing everything right and kids pushing them away for a season.

If you are a parent whose child is estranged or has severed rela-tionships for any reason, don't isolate yourself or walk the path alone. Talk to your spouse. Support each other rather than work against each other in your individual pain. Reach out to a support group, trusted friends, or a counselor with whom you can process feelings, express grief, and receive support. Your emotional health is important for you, your marriage, and the other kids you're still parenting. Take care of yourself. Set boundaries where needed and practice self-care.

Take heart—God is still the author of your story. The prodigal son was an estranged son. God redeems and creates good things after seasons of desolation and destruction. Even though Job lost everything he loved and valued, God restored his health, a new family, and a time of goodness at the end of his life. God has not abandoned you if you are estranged from your child or if there's deep pain in your family. Run to him. Fight the battle in prayer, but also let others join that fight, just as Aaron and Hur supported Moses as he watched Joshua fight the Amalekites (Exodus 17:12).

Remember, you are a warrior fighting a battle for your family. Your child is not your enemy. Your adversary is the enemy of God, who is attacking your family. Put on your armor, let Christ be your shield, and have hope in Jesus, the restorer and redeemer.

We can have confidence that God is working for our healing and for the healing of our children. Instead of being distraught at your current circumstances, look ahead at the story God is writing, though you don't yet know the outcome. Jesus is on the other side of your circumstances. Look up! Fix your eyes on him. Trust that God continues to restore and redeem the years of pain and heartache.

BUILDING UP
and letting go

Lord, thank you that you never fail me when my kids mess up or when I sin. Help me not to worry about what others think but to focus on what's best for my child and family. Equip me to be more honest with myself and others. Thank you for being the restorer and redeemer. Amen.

1. What speaks to you most in this chapter?

2. Who are the safe people in your life to talk to?

3. What parenting truths do you need to hear the most?

4. How can you apply that truth to your life right now?

14

The Family
That Prays Together

*Faith is confidence in what we hope for and assurance about what
we do not see.*
—HEBREWS 11:1

I sat outside my child's bedroom door, praying the type of prayer
where you think your heart is going to fall out of your chest
because it hurts so badly. Ron was in the room talking to one of
our teens who was angry and hurt at a situation over which we
had no control. As I heard our teen cry and verbalize his hurt, I
wanted to rush in and save him.

But I wasn't the person to make it better for him.

Only God could. I really *needed* God to be with my child. And
I needed the assurance that God was with him.

It's a scene that has happened over and over again for me, as a
mom of teens and young adults. Laying your children at the feet
of Jesus is the only place to go when you give up control and take
your hands off your kids. In fact, as your kids grow up, prayer and
faith really are the only resources you have, because most other
things are out of your control.

It's the real deal of trust and faith: not knowing what the outcome is going to be and asking God to meet the needs of your kids.

How do you release that grip on your child's life, trusting God with the rest of her story that you're not writing anymore?

One word—prayer. Let's look at the power of prayer in relinquishing control, letting go, and making it through difficult circumstances.

FAITH AND PRAYER | My father-in-law's prayers over his family in the last days of his life changed my commitment to prayer as a parent. As Ron and I reflected over the godly heritage his mom and dad left, we wondered how many things we were spared because his parents were prayer warriors. Even in midlife, when your parents pray for you, you feel at peace knowing you're not alone and that your parents are still there, protecting and guiding.

True confession, though: my prayer life can be sporadic when life is busy and things are good. When those storms come, though, we get serious about prayer real quick, don't we? We pray more fervently because we can't change, fix, or affect the situation. However, prayer is only one part of the equation. Prayer coupled with faith releases children from our hands into the hands of the heavenly Father. "Faith is confidence in what we hope for and assurance about what we do not see," Hebrews 11:1 says.

Philippians 4:6-7 says that you are not to be anxious about anything but that you are to "in every situation, by prayer and petition, with thanksgiving, present your requests to God." Then God's peace, which "transcends all understanding, will guard your hearts and your minds in Christ Jesus."

Do you need peace guarding your heart and mind when it comes to your kids? I sure do.

Parents, we are to pray about *anything*. We're to bring our fears, heartache, and the deepest parent pain to the Lord. Scripture commands us to pray without ceasing (1 Thessalonians 5:17), to pray expectantly (Matthew 6:5-14), to pray about everything (Philippians 4:6), and to pray in faith through a personal relationship with Christ (Hebrews 11:6).

One Bible story that strengthens my faith is that of Abraham in Genesis 21–22. Scripture doesn't mention Abraham's prayers, but his actions model how to respond when we don't understand our circumstances. I turn to this passage when worried or anxious for the outcome of a situation in my child's life.

In Genesis 22, God commands Abraham to offer his son Isaac as a sacrifice to him. That's not the directive I'd want to receive from God. You can imagine Abraham's confusion at the command and his dilemma: Should he obey God or not?

Have you ever been confused at what is happening in your child's life? Have you wondered why God allows certain things to happen? I'm sure Abraham felt that way. How could God ask him to kill his long-awaited son as an offering to him? Those are real questions!

It didn't make sense, yet Abraham obeyed. He trusted God on the basis of God's goodness and character. When God didn't make sense, instead of walking *away* from God and taking things into his own hands, Abraham walked toward God, trusting God would provide.

Here's a snippet of the powerful scene in Genesis 22:7-8:

> "Father?"
>
> "Yes, my son?" Abraham replied
>
> "The fire and wood are here," Isaac said, "but where is the lamb for the burnt offering?"
>
> Abraham answered, "God himself will provide the lamb for the burnt offering, my son." And the two of them went on together.

I know the risk of trusting God when I have no answers, of telling my kids he'll provide when I don't know how. But if Abraham could trust God's loving character when he obediently laid his child on the altar, then so can I. So can you.

God *will* provide for our kids when we offer them on the altar of prayer.

But we have to take our hands off and trust God. What would it have looked like if Abraham had taken things into his own hands? His responses may have sounded like: "Isaac, just in case

God doesn't provide, I'm going to take this lamb along." "Isaac, come down from that altar. God's not going to follow through."

Abraham's disbelief would have robbed God of the opportunity to work in a profound way. If Abraham had taken control of the situation, he would have deprived himself of the opportunity to trust God more deeply. We do the same when we take things in our own hands when God doesn't come through on our timetable.

Can God provide for your children and their situations in ways you can't imagine? Yes! Sometimes the answer to your child's questions for unknown outcomes will be "I don't know how, but God is going to provide."

TRUSTING GOD AND HIS CHARACTER | I was a storyteller for vacation Bible school at our church during the summer before I started teaching. I had been a stay-at-home mom for more than a decade, and that summer I was struggling with the idea of giving up control of my younger two kids, who would be staying with a babysitter in our home. The Scripture verse for vacation Bible school was Philippians 4:19, "And my God will meet all of your needs according to the riches of his glory in Christ Jesus." For five nights that week, I taught kids how God would provide for their every need. I was challenged to believe what I was teaching. God was teaching me that he would provide for my toddler's and preschooler's emotional needs as I transitioned to full-time work. It was the first time I really trusted God with my kids in an area in which I had no control.

God faithfully provided. Drew and Ethan adjusted to our new life, as did I. God showed me he *does* provide for the physical, emotional, and spiritual needs of my family. This promise increases my faith because I have to believe God knows my child's needs better than I do.

The greatest tools you have as a parent are prayer and faith. We are often afraid to proclaim faith when praying, because it implies that answered prayer is contingent on our faith. We face disappointment when God doesn't answer the way we asked. But faith is trusting that God's character isn't based on life's circumstances and outcomes. Faith is believing God is meeting the needs of people in a difficult situation even when we don't see it.

When Jenna was eight years old, Ron's mom was taken to the hospital after having outpatient knee surgery the day before. Jenna asked, "Is Grandma going to be okay?" I hesitated to answer with a simple yes. I wondered what it would do to Jenna's young faith if Grandma wasn't okay. Something prevented me from flippantly praying that Grandma would be fine.

I told Jenna I didn't know if Grandma would be okay. As we prayed together, I asked God for his will to be done. We thanked God that he was in control.

By the time Ron and I got to the hospital, his mom had passed away from a blood clot that had traveled to her lungs. Everything I thought I knew about God's character was shattered in that moment. How could he be good when the woman we loved so much was taken from us this way? It was a simple outpatient procedure! I had to tell myself that God was the same in that moment as he had been the day before. God was still good, loving, faithful, compassionate, slow to anger and abounding in love, as Psalm 145:8 says, though our circumstances were painful.

I believe the Holy Spirit prevented me from praying a quick, flippant prayer with Jenna that evening. Instead, we had asked God to be in control and for God's will to be done. That prayer was answered, though it wasn't the outcome I anticipated. People aren't supposed to die from complications from an outpatient procedure. Nor are other tragedies supposed to happen to families who love God—or so we think.

I'm sure you've had similar thoughts and experiences. That experience taught me that God's character doesn't change when our circumstances are no longer good. I was forced to have faith in God rather than in the circumstances.

Circumstantial faith will always be disappointing, wishy-washy, and uncertain. God and his character *do not* change (Malachi 3:6). Abraham knew God was still the same on the mountain as he was in the valley. God is the only thing we are sure of when our circumstances tell us otherwise.

Being a Christian doesn't exclude us or our kids from pain. Prayer and faith are essential to get us through.

I've found there are two types of significant prayers: prayer *for* our children and prayer *with* our children. Partnered with these prayers is Abrahamic faith: trusting that God will provide for their needs.

PRAYING *FOR* YOUR CHILDREN | There are two dimensions of a parent's prayer. The first is your position as the guardian who prays over your child. Throughout Scripture, we see parents interceding for the needs of their children. Examples of these are the widows in 1 Kings 17 and 2 Kings 4 who came to the prophets, as well as the parent in Matthew 9 who came to Jesus. In Matthew 19:14, Jesus directed the disciples to bring the children to him. His command is no different to us today.

You and I are prayer warriors positioned under the Builder and Protector of the family. It's a responsibility uniquely ours. If your kids are not praying for their needs, then who is bringing them before the Father? Philippians 4:6-7 gives us the command and promise of prayer: "Do not be anxious about anything, but in every situation, by prayer and petition, with thanksgiving, present your requests to God. And the peace of God, which transcends all understanding, will guard your hearts and your minds in Christ Jesus."

If prayer were the only resource you had in parenting, would you use it to its full potential? Different situations require different types of prayer. Here are six types of prayer a parent can pray.

Preventive prayers. Preventive prayers are prayed ahead of a situation. These are things you hope to see fulfilled in the life of your child. Prayers for protection, a godly spouse, health, safety, a good job: these prayers bring before God's throne needs for your child's future.

Specific need prayers. These prayers are the most common— decisions about college, choices, morals, relationships, and so on. However, we often try to control these areas before we pray about them. The enemy distracts us by questioning God's involvement in the details of our child's life. God *is* involved. He desires to move in a mighty way—but we need to ask him (James 5:13-16).

Praise and thanksgiving prayers. In the busyness of parenting, you can forget prayers of praise. Praise and thanksgiving are even more challenging when you're waiting for prayers to be answered or when you feel that God has forgotten or abandoned you or your child. The enemy wants you to doubt God's presence when he appears silent. Faith, on the other hand, says, "I will believe you, God, even when I don't see the answer." In times of waiting for God's answer, praise God for who he is and what he is doing in your child's life even though you don't see it.

Scriptural prayers of promise. Prayers of faith as mentioned above are often done by taking Scripture or promises in Scripture and praying them to God. I pray Philippians 4:19 when I need God to simply meet a child's needs. Psalm 10 is just one of many psalms you can also pray in these situations. Praying Scripture is often the place to start when you're at a loss of how to pray.

Scriptural prayers of blessing. Prayers of blessing invite God's favor and goodness on your child. Praying blessing from Scripture offers back to God his truth and desires for them. One Scripture I pray is that my kids will grow in wisdom and in favor with God and others, as Jesus and Samuel did (Luke 2:40, 52; 1 Samuel 2:26).

Intercessory prayers. Interceding is intervening and petitioning on your child's behalf in a persistent, steadfast manner. You go to God often, reminding him of the needs of your child, of past prayers, of God's promises, his character, and of the power he has to change the situation. Jesus does not ignore the petitions of his children. In the Luke 18:1-8 parable of the persistent widow, Jesus says we should pray and not give up, and says that he brings about justice for his chosen ones who cry out day and night. Matthew 15:21-28 also tells the story of a woman who begged Jesus to heal her daughter even after Jesus dismissed her request. She was rewarded explicitly for her *faith*.

Our teens and young adults need us interceding. Prayer is the most powerful and influential responsibility we have in their lives.

PRAYING *WITH* YOUR CHILDREN | The second dimension of your prayer life as a parent is praying *with* your children. In this position, you are more than just a guardian; you are modeling, strengthening, and pouring into them. Praying with your teen or young adult strengthens her faith, gives her courage, and makes God personal to her.

Teens want authenticity. It makes a deep impression on them when you bring their needs before God. They look to you for real faith whether you think they do or not. Hearing you pray brings comfort and security. It shows you care about them and that *your* faith is real because they see it in action.

How can you pray *with* your kids?

- Praise God for what he has done, *is* doing, and will do in your young person's life.
- Pray Scripture over a situation. It shows your teen that God's Word is relevant to his life. When someone needs courage, my favorite Scripture is Joshua 1.
- When you aren't sure how to pray, ask God to meet your child's needs and to give her a peace that passes all understanding, as Philippians 4:7 and 19 say.
- Simply talk to God from your heart.
- Pray with your kids about big decisions, before an event when they're nervous, and about relationships and other concerns.

Your teen or young adult knows you're on his team when you pray with him. When he shares his struggles, don't diminish his feelings. Instead, honor them. Praying with your child models the intimacy of a personal relationship: you with him, you with God, and him with God. It shows your child that you see and know him.

A NOTE OF CAUTION | There are some situations that require more than prayer. If your child is struggling with mental illness, depression, suicidal thoughts, toxic relationships, social problems, self-harm, rebellion, sexual promiscuity, pornography, addiction, victimization, or other harming behaviors, professional help should be sought in addition to prayer. Don't minimize these situations.

Also, before praying with your teen or young adult, ask for permission. Ask, "Can we pray about this?" or "Do you mind if I pray with you?" This respects children's autonomy and doesn't force unwanted prayer on them. If your relationship with your child is rocky, prayer can feel intrusive, violating, or hypocritical. It could hinder your relationship with her and her relationship with God if it's forced on her. Show your child honor and respect by asking. If her answer is no, follow through with restraint.

If your child says yes, recognize the special moment it is. She's letting you into a small part of her world. It's a sacred place of intimacy that should be treated as a gift.

PRAYING AS A FAMILY | During the years of conflict and strife in our home, Ron and I were challenged by a message to develop a time for the family to connect. We designated Sunday evenings as a time for our family to come together for prayer, conversation, and often a devotional. It only lasts about ten to twenty minutes. When we started, the older teens thought it was lame. It has sometimes been awkward. But as our kids have started leaving the nest, this family time has become significant.

Prayer is an integral part of this time. We pray over the events or prayer requests the kids have for the upcoming week. We pray a blessing over each child at the beginning of the school year or when college kids leave to go back for a new semester. We pray for the family members who aren't with us because they're in college or living on their own now.

Prayer binds your family together through adversity. It is the foundation when your family is changing, when kids move away, and when the storms of life hit hard.

Prayer changed the climate in our home when our family was falling apart. The spiritual battle was very evident. When you do battle in the spiritual realm for the deep needs in a family, God provides. Too often we give up because we only see what's in front of us. God wants us to look up, to lift up and offer up our deepest needs, greatest joys, and intangible faith for our family.

Laying your child on the altar means laying down your control, worry, fears, and practical expectations. It means putting your child at the feet of Jesus in prayer. You take a position of extraordinary faith, trusting that God himself will provide.

BUILDING UP
and letting go

Father, thank you for being steadfast and never-changing. Thank you for providing when I don't know how you will. Equip me to trust you on the basis of your character, not the circumstances. Teach me to pray with expectant faith for the lives of my children. Amen.

1. What obstacles do you have in bringing your kids' simple and difficult needs to God?

2. What are things you can praise God for in the life of your family?

3. What things do you know to be true about God's character?

4. What is one principle you can apply to your prayer life now?

15

Take Care of You

And let us run with perseverance the race marked out for us, fixing our eyes on Jesus, the pioneer and perfecter of faith.
—HEBREWS 12:1-2

It was the last year with two kids at home, and I was in denial. Drew was a high school senior, and Ethan was a freshman. Our family had slowly dwindled—four kids, three kids, two kids. Soon it would be just one.

Then none.

We were *here*, approaching the final stretch of our childrearing years. My emotions were all over the place. I posted sappy pictures on social media about how fast my kids were growing up.

I was *her*—the woman avoiding the reality that midlife and empty nest were on the horizon. When I was a young mom, I judged women like me. I thought they were lame and sappy as they oozed over their kids who were growing up and moving on.

And here I was.

I didn't want my kids to grow up. I was oozy and sappy and every other stereotype of a middle-aged woman whose kids are leaving home. I wanted to walk these years of transition with grace. Instead, I felt like an alien in my body and home.

I told myself this is part of life, and all mothers must go through this. But I wondered if anyone else felt this vulnerable and emotional with kids both in and out of the nest.

My hang-up wasn't being sentimental; it was losing sight of letting go. Though your head knows that goal, daily life sweeps it away. With each child you release, the empty nest gets closer and closer, and you want to turn back full force.

When I was a kid, my sisters and I made whirlpools in our above-ground pool. First we'd walk in one direction, making a strong current which would eventually carry us with it. Then we'd turn around and walk against the flow. It was difficult to walk in the opposite direction. You couldn't move forward. All your energy was pushing against the current.

That's what I was doing. I was pushing against the natural order of life. I was stuck looking back, trying to slow down the flow of life as my kids swept toward adulthood. Only this current you can't change. You can't freeze time or prevent your kids from growing up. Working against it makes you lose out on what's happening now, enjoying each child at their current stage.

You have to walk *with* life's changes, not against them. Otherwise you are trying to hold on to something that's slipping through your fingers.

But not only are your kids changing; you're changing too. As you prepare your kids to fledge the nest, you're preparing your own wings for flight and independence. That's hard to do if you're running on empty, emotionally depleted, and not meeting your needs in the here and now.

WHAT ABOUT ME? | Two things happen as your kids leave: they gain independence from you and you gain independence from them. Initially, this change doesn't feel good. You've poured your heart into each child for eighteen or so years, and in many ways you're saying goodbye: goodbye to being an active part of her daily life, to fixing things that can be fixed, to enjoying her childhood, to having your hand on her, and to knowing where she is and that she's okay.

You're letting go with one hand while trying to hold on with the other. The more you hold on, the more it feels like your child is being ripped away. While she walks away, part of you goes with her.

And it hurts. Really, it physically hurts some days. The emptiness. The loss. The ache in your heart no one in your family is experiencing the way you are. Your journey is different from your child's and your spouse's. The wound that remains when your child separates can be raw. Other than significant milestones like graduations or weddings, my husband hasn't felt the sadness or emotions I've had in letting each child go. That makes it hard to share my journey at times, because he doesn't understand.

While you can't take away the sadness, you can prepare yourself so the longings and the holes are filled with healthy things. It's important you take care of yourself during this transitional phase. As your kids fledge, you're also learning to fly in a new direction.

Have you thought about *your* goals for the empty-nest years? More specifically, have you thought about life outside of your kids? That's the real question. It's frightening when you no longer take care of or influence your kids. When your well-being, happiness, and self-worth are wrapped up in parenting, these things can slip away along with your children. Even when you've actively invested in activities and interests beyond your kids, there is still a loss.

Your parenting roles are shifting and yet you may feel caught between the past and the future. Rather than spend your energy looking back, take care of yourself and embrace what's in front of you *now*.

THE BLESSING OF NOW | It took most of Drew's senior year for me to embrace the here and now. It was sobering when I realized the sadness I felt that year was more about *me* than about Drew's senior milestones.

I was caught up in my own losses instead of celebrating his achievements, such as his last ball game and last awards banquet. It's eye-opening to see your own selfishness.

As mothers, we spend most of our parenting years proving to ourselves we *aren't* selfish. We nurture and give without much praise or acknowledgment. Our feelings get trampled on and disrespected (especially by high school seniors!). You may feel like the least-valued person in the house, yet you long for your kids to be thankful for who you are and what you do for them.

Teens, however, won't tell you how great you are. In fact, most of their time is spent pushing you away—even though they still need you, sometimes more than ever. Your high schooler gets dumped by his girlfriend. Your college student struggles with depression. Your middle schooler does inappropriate things on her phone. You pour yourself out when they struggle, and rarely get a thank you in return.

Rearing your kids has become your expertise. Saying goodbye to this role is a huge transition. When distracted by the loss or nostalgia of the past, you can miss what's in front of you, along with enjoying both significant and ordinary events. Graduations, engagements, weddings, and proms: sometimes these events happen simultaneously. A friend recently had two weddings and a high school graduation all within four weeks' time.

Sound exhausting? Some days it is. Some days you'll cry tears of both grief and joy, and other emotions you aren't even aware of.

Enjoying the present is a choice. So is taking care of yourself. It's your new order of business as you celebrate and grieve all at the same time.

TAKING CARE OF BUSINESS | For a long time I lived for the next school year, the next sports season, the next stage, thinking problems would be fixed in the *next* season of family life. The next season, eventually, is a house without kids.

Waiting for the next season to fix our family's problems only prolonged unhealthy behavior. Change in our family happened when I looked at my needs and made necessary changes by pursuing self-care. No matter what parenting mess you may find yourself in, there is hope. If there are problems you've identified throughout our discussions, I encourage you to take care of yourself and face what needs to change.

I've referred to Joel 2 several times because it's a chapter of encouragement for parents needing hope and redemption. Joel 2 is a story of God's promised redemption to Israel after destruction and loss. However, God required confession and repentance before restoration. Confession and repentance hold us accountable for our stuff; they prevent us from laying blame anywhere else. I had to confess that, out of exhaustion, my critical, angry, and reactionary responses were hurting our family. Repentance meant I had to focus on the things only I could change before Jenna left for college. Change involves risks. For me, taking care of myself and dealing with unhealthy behavior were the only things I could control. A change in lifestyle was the only answer for the mess we were living in.

Two weeks after I resigned from teaching, redemption began. In a conversation between Jenna and I, a new dialogue happened. She talked to me about a personal issue and I listened and responded instead of reacting. When she left the room, there was a peaceful presence in our home that was almost tangible. Jesus *was* with us. God's restoration in our family had begun. Hope for healing had arrived.

God *is* the redeemer of the years the locusts have eaten, even in parenting. But God doesn't do the work on his own. He doesn't change your family by osmosis. Change happens by choice when you allow Jesus Christ to do what you can't do yourself.

GOD'S PROMISES | Three years after I quit teaching, we took our last family vacation with all four kids. They were ages twenty, seventeen, fourteen, and twelve. The kids unanimously requested that we go to the Focus on the Family headquarters in Colorado Springs, Colorado. They wanted to see Whit's End—a re-creation of the popular soda shop hangout in the fictional story series Adventures in Odyssey. I had started buying Adventures in Odyssey audio stories as gifts for our kids when they were young, and the younger kids still listened to them.

Until we made that trip, I had no idea how those faith-based stories had influenced and bonded our kids together.

When we reached our destination, we went to the lower-level exhibit, which was filled with the Whit's End Soda Shop, life-sized characters, and activities for kids which centered on the stories. My Bigs were taking in everything, walking around and pointing at things while much younger kids were running all around them. I overheard Mark, age seventeen, tell Jenna, "This is like reliving our entire childhood."

I looked at the younger families amid my own, and my heart ached. Though our family was healing, the grief and regret over the hurt of the past was still fresh. I longed for the days when my kids were younger, before pain entered our home.

But in the middle of my thoughts, other scenes from our family life flashed in my mind. Instead of seeing only the bad times, I saw the good. Moments of peace and love, and relationships we built. In God's grace, he replaced grief with goodness that I had been unable to see on my own. I felt that familiar, peaceful presence of God.

When the kids got on the elevator to leave the basement floor, I remained behind. I needed a few minutes alone, knowing a flood of tears was about to erupt. As I witnessed all of them smiling and laughing in the elevator, a voice inside me said, "It is finished." I knew God was confirming that the years the locusts had eaten were over. That hurtful chapter in our family life was done.

God's faithfulness continues to heal each season in our family's journey. He will do the same for you.

REALITY CHECK | There's a common saying about parenting: "It's not what's taught; it's what's caught." It's true. What you live in front of your kids, day in and day out, is the truth they receive about life, themselves, the world, and priorities. The childrearing years go so fast you often don't realize the mess you're in until you're stuck and don't know how to get out.

We don't get do-overs in parenting. We only have now. Your emotional and mental health affects your kids. Marital conflict, strife between siblings, and problems of individual kids also affect the family. Daily actions speak most to your children. How is your emotional health or that of your family? Is there something you need to take care of?

We need to be healthy and emotionally available because our teens need us. We can't see or hear what our teens need when our energy is absorbed by our own issues and problems. Though your teen might be shutting you out, they still need you engaged in their life.

Stay focused. The enemy wants to distract you. Distraction is the new drug for parents in the twenty-first century. Social media, careers, busyness, and materialism take your attention away from family, priorities, emotional health, and the climate of home. These things pull you away from Christ, preventing him from being the Master Builder.

Fix your eyes on Jesus. He's waiting for you to hand over control of your time, energy, and emotional needs and those of your children. You and I mess things up when we do it alone.

Take care of yourself by being honest with God about your hurts, unhealthy behavior, attitudes, or words. Make space in your jam-packed schedule to connect with him—through prayer, Scripture, journaling, or other reflective tools. Humble yourself to reassess priorities, change behavior, or heal your hurts, even if it requires professional help.

The Holy Spirit prompted and convicted me about changing my unhealthy behavior. He made me aware of how my sharp words affected my kids. He humbled me to ask them for forgiveness when I needed to. He removed anger and made me more patient. I had to yield to these promptings, though.

I had to choose to let him change me.

Surrendering your emotions, behaviors, priorities, and relationships to God is vital to the health and security of your family. Let God equip you with his strength. Take care of you by taking care of your stuff.

PRACTICAL SELF-CARE | Self-care doesn't have to be as drastic as switching jobs or dealing with major emotional issues. In many cases, like mine, lack of self-care simply pushes underlying issues to the surface. So how do you take care of yourself so you can be a healthy parent today?

- Make self-care a lifestyle habit. Once you figure out the healthiest ways to implement self-care, make them a priority for a lifetime.
- Know your limits. Understand what causes you the most stress and establish boundaries. Say no or "not now" to things or people who deplete you during this season.
- Don't worry about what others think.
- Know your needs by admitting you have them. A key question I ask clients is, "What do you need?" Answering that question defines your short-term and long-term needs. Your needs vary according to each season of your family life or according to your current struggle. When you feel stuck, depleted, anxious, or stressed, ask yourself that question.
- Communicate your needs to your spouse. This is tough if you and your spouse are not on the same page or if you feel that he won't understand. He may not. It's still important to advocate for yourself.
- Talk with your kids about your needs. One of the blessings of older children is their capacity to see beyond themselves. Communicate your needs to them so they're aware of when you need a break or how they can help with external stresses. I often tell my kids when I need a day away for my own mental health.
- Find practical tools to meet your needs. It might be hiring a cleaning service, having a date with your spouse, a night out with friends, or a weekend away by yourself. Or it might be seeking support through a counselor or life coach. Lifestyle changes might be the long-term solution—a change in job, the addition of a hobby, or doing something fun that's just for you—no kids allowed!
- Invest in your relationship with Christ.

- Give yourself grace (there's a whole chapter on that coming up).

Self-care is not selfish. Jesus pulled away for solitude and time with his Father. It's okay to take care of you.

BUILDING UP
and letting go

Jesus, thank you for being the model of self-care. Thank you that you are the provider of our every need in each season. Equip me to see things I need to change so I can be more present with our family now. Help me not to look behind or too far ahead and miss the now. Amen.

1. What do you identify with in the chapter?

2. What stuff do you need to take care of that's hindering you from fully enjoying your family now?

3. What is difficult to you about self-care?

4. What's one self-care principle you can apply now?

16

Shut the Door
on Your Way Out

There is a time for everything, and a season for every activity under the heavens.
—ECCLESIASTES 3:1

The time had come. Ethan was starting his sophomore year of high school and was now the sole kid in the house after twenty-two years. For three weeks in a row, I said goodbye to his older siblings, one by one, as they embarked on new experiences. Drew and Mark moved to their respective colleges for their freshman and senior years, and Jenna was on the mission field.

A lot of moments caught me off guard. I'd walk by one of the kids' empty bedrooms and the emptiness matched the state of my heart. I'd fill out the school picture form, noting how strange it was to fill out paperwork for only one kid. I'd tear up at the sight of the child-sized bat Drew used during Little League in the pile of things Ron was taking to Goodwill.

Sentimental feelings, honestly, aren't ones I've felt too often in a house full of eye-rolling, "Mom, you're so stupid," teens and young adults. I had several moments in the months leading up to the Big Departure in which I couldn't wait to get the kids out the door. That's the emotional roller coaster of living with teens and young adults transitioning to independence. One day you think they're the greatest thing on the planet, and the next day you're counting down the days until they leave.

Still weepy and sullen over the kids being gone, I was excited when one of the college boys came home unexpectedly for Labor Day weekend. His roommate and friends had gone home for the holiday, so he came home too.

He hadn't been home for more than a few hours when a simple question I asked brought that "Mom, get off my back!" response. The sad mom switch flipped pretty quickly. Suddenly, I wasn't so weepy anymore.

I had quickly forgotten that disrespectful and rude comments often accompany kids ready to be on their own. They don't like being questioned about their business or being told what to do.

I was reminded that *there is a time* for young adults to leave the nest. It's God's natural order of things. While I didn't welcome College Boy's snarky remarks, it was a quick fix for my mood.

Fledging happens because there's a definite time for the kids to leave the nest. The challenge is to get the fledglings out at the proper time while still caring for those not yet ready to fly.

QUEST FOR INDEPENDENCE | Ecclesiastes 3 reminds us there's a time for everything in the life cycle. This includes kids leaving at the appropriate time. Kids naturally start pushing their independence, but each one does it differently. Sometimes it makes your head spin. The fledging season stretches you, the mom, as you're helping one child fly out of that nest while still raising others.

That "don't tell me what to do" attitude starts around age twelve, give or take a year or two. It grows as kids move toward adulthood. Natural development means kids start to think, "I'm old enough to make my own decisions," but their brains aren't fully developed yet. The battle for independence and autonomy is one you can expect. Being aware of the normalcy and the need for independence helps with the frustration and hurt a parent can feel during the process.

Ages fourteen, seventeen, and last-semester seniors are the ages I dislike the most. With each of my kids, these were the ages where disrespect seemed the worst. But these attitudes are part of the separating process. Adolescence is when kids crave independence, want to make decisions, and have control in their lives. There's a gradual line of control, influence, and independence that widens as kids transition to adulthood. There's also a temptation to keep the parent-child relationship stagnant as teens make the passage from high school to post–high school life. But the relationship needs to change for a healthy transition.

Today's culture enables helicopter parents and extended young adulthood. In generations past, kids were expected to have independence and forge their way into their new adult lives, with parents supporting them but stepping back. Now there's a new phenomenon of parents taking care of young adult children as they did when those kids were teens, resulting in an inappropriately extended childhood. While housing a young adult is one thing, caring for young adults and making decisions for them the way you did when they were teens hinders their natural transition to adulthood.

The tension between independence and growing up doesn't just go away at high school graduation. It continues as young people find their way in their new world, whether they work and live at home or go to college. Parental frustration is normal when kids live with you but are not under your childrearing authority anymore. If your adult son or daughter lives at home for a period, whether while in college or in the workforce, it's important to make the distinction that you're not parenting that child the way you did when he or she was a minor. They are adults, no matter how they are living, and they gain respect for themselves and you when they are treated as adults. Revisit those questions in the earlier chapters on giving up control, setting boundaries, and not stealing the struggle—they are important for navigating the tension between independence and letting go.

THE BOOMERANG KID | "And then your kids come back . . ."
I've heard parents say when I share the subject of this book with
them. What they're referring to is the "boomerang kid": adult
kids, single or married, some with children, who move back home.

According to a 2014 Pew Research Center study, young adults
ages eighteen to thirty-four are more likely to be living with their
parents than young adults in any other time since 1880.[1] Economic
factors and a decline in romantic relationships and marriage were
cited as primary reasons for this trend.

Younger kids are affected when an adult sibling moves home.
We went through this transition for the year before Jenna moved
to the mission field. Your family changes with a boomerang kid.
But their circumstances still don't change the fact that God's ultimate plan includes their independence and autonomy. Here are a
few things to consider if you find yourself with a boomerang kid:

- Your primary focus should be on any minor kids you're still
  raising. Their lives should not be majorly interrupted by the
  young adult moving home. They are still kids and need to
  have their time with friends and mom and dad, as well as
  private space, especially during adolescence.
- Set clear expectations with the adult child moving home.
  Look at the questions in chapter 7 for guidelines of how
  living together will work while adult children are in your
  home, especially regarding younger siblings.
- Don't allow the adult child to treat younger children with
  contempt or disrespect.
- Set boundaries, guard against entitlement, and don't enable
  bad decisions or poor behavior.
- Don't do things for your adult kids that they should do for
  themselves. If they'd be doing it on their own in an apartment, they should be doing it at home too.

---

1. Richard Fry, "For First Time in Modern Era, Living with Parents Edges Out Other
Living Arrangements for 18- to 34-Year-Olds," Pew Research Center, May 24, 2016,
http://www.pewsocialtrends.org/2016/05/24/for-first-time-in-modern-era-living-with-
parents-edges-out-other-living-arrangements-for-18-to-34-year-olds/.

- Assess the reasons your young adult has moved home, and have a plan and projected timeline for her to be on her own. Young adults move home for a variety of reasons—to save money, to pay off college debt, or because of a crisis. Many young adults live at home because they don't know what they want to do with their lives or because they're indecisive about a career path or long-term goals. This isn't a reason for them to stay home indefinitely. They can work and live in an apartment while they figure that out.

It's important to mention that different cultures have different expectations. In many cultures, it's acceptable for young adults to live at home until they marry. Similar principles of balance and autonomy still apply, but these things may look different within particular cultural contexts or family situations.

No matter the reason a young person lives at home after high school, the goal is for him to be developmentally prepared for the flight path God has for him. Kids can't develop strong wings if those muscles aren't used.

Autonomy and independence, however, are not determined by proximity. They are characteristics of growth. For example, an adult child may live far away from home but still be emotionally, practically (as in calling whenever she has car problems), or financially tied to her parents in an unhealthy way. This might be true even if she is married with children. In these cases, fledging hasn't really occurred, because proper wing feathers haven't been developed. Parents have enabled a dependent relationship similar to that of childhood.

On the other hand, an adult child living in the parents' home for financial or cultural reasons may have an appropriate balance of emotional, physical, and financial independence and autonomy. I've seen this done well, and it can be beneficial in particular circumstances.

If your young adult is home because of personal crisis—such as medical or mental health issues, addiction, an unhealthy relationship, or abuse—let home be a safe place for him while he receives professional treatment and gets on his feet. At the same time, be aware that this scenario can also lead to enabling, codependency, toxicity, and lack of boundaries. Once an adult is out of crisis, move him toward independence. He is responsible for his choices, treatment, and quality of life, even if these choices are not what you want to see for him.

Because toxic siblings in the house affect younger kids, the interests of the underage kids should be *first* after the immediate boomerang crisis is over. If the boomerang child is in constant crisis and isn't taking responsibility for her situation and it's affecting younger siblings, other plans for the adult should be considered. The choices of an unhealthy and toxic sibling should not define the growing-up years of minor children.

In the toughest of situations, you may have to choose between the health of your minor children and the poor choices of your young adult. These are hard decisions to make. But your younger kids are still *children*. Adult kids make adult choices and can be responsible for the consequences. This requires tough love.

They are capable of "adulting" even if they don't appear to be. Their biological clock says so. They'll figure it out, one way or another.

PARENTING ON AUTOPILOT | You may not have boomerangs at home. Maybe you have just one kid left at home and you already feel free! Life is nice in many respects when you have just your youngest at home. But beware of the temptation to parent on autopilot, letting that youngest child or children raise themselves.

I remember a response by a student to a writing assignment I gave when teaching high school sociology. Missy, a high school senior, was the youngest child of older parents, and there was a large age gap between her and her older siblings. In her essay, she reported how her parents didn't have any curfew for her, were frequently away from home, and didn't check up on her while she openly partied in their absence. She wrote, "They don't care what I do. I wish they did."

That response has always stuck with me. Disengaged parenting can harm kids.

Remaining as fully engaged with your youngest child or children as you did with your older kids can be a struggle. You gain your own sense of independence and freedom with each child who leaves. I've easily slipped into autopilot parenting with my younger teens. Like other stages of parenting, this stage requires knowing your limits, your child's needs, and the current needs of the family. There's not a one-size-fits-all explanation for how this works for each family, and reassessment is necessary.

After Jenna and Mark were both in college, I found a nice equilibrium with just Drew and Ethan at home. They were in high school and junior high. I was working, writing, and speaking more, while still balancing their busy sports schedules. I liked my new world with fewer demands of time and energy than I'd had when all four kids were at home. Simple things like grocery shopping and laundry were not as cumbersome. I didn't want that sense of ease interrupted.

The year after Jenna graduated from college, she pursued her dream of being a full-time missionary. It was exciting to see her connect with a mission agency that matched her passion for orphan care. She had lived in another state since leaving for college, and she moved home for a year before going to the mission field to raise financial support. I was excited to have Jenna home for a while before she left for Mexico. I also realized how much our household would change and what big things were on the horizon for the younger boys. Drew would be a senior that year and Ethan a freshman. Lots of firsts and lasts for both of them. With just two kids at home, I was often parenting on autopilot. Teen boys don't demand much except clean clothes and a stocked refrigerator. I could handle that.

But I was still *raising* them. I needed to be as faithful, committed, and emotionally available to them as I had been to Jenna and Mark when they were teens. I also needed to support Jenna in different ways as she prepared to be a missionary.

I couldn't do all of that and keep up my professional commitments without being stretched thin. I made adjustments to both my personal and professional schedule during those months Jenna was home, saying no to certain things so I could appropriately engage with each child as needed.

The time went incredibly fast, and it was filled with unexpected events and stresses we couldn't have anticipated. Instead of walking the tightrope of "I'm too busy," I was able to be present for some important moments with each of the kids.

I'm so glad I made the adjustments.

THE BALANCING ACT | Preparing each child for independence and autonomy is a balancing act. Your teens need you to be fully invested, to be that strong warrior all the way to the end of their childhood experiences, though they may not show it. As rude as their behavior may be as they assert their independence, they need you as their parent. They still need boundaries, nurture, and guidance even though they look, sound, and feel like adults.

Parenting young adults is a different balancing act than parenting teens because the level of independence and autonomy is different. It, too, requires emotional energy and a learning curve on your part. It involves letting your children figure things out while holding them accountable, supporting them but standing back. The transition, like any other, involves assessment and adjustments as needed.

Boundaries, freedom, support, and transition: these parenting struggles ebb and flow through the lifespan. Independence is good. Watching from the sidelines is new, different, and surreal in many ways.

Each of us will eventually see our little boy or girl walk out the door with that huge suitcase. In your eyes, they will always be your baby.

With each child you let go, there are growing pains. But with God as your strength, you'll figure it out too.

BUILDING UP
and letting go

Father, equip me for the challenges I'm facing with my child. Help me have the strength and stamina to be fully engaged until each of the children graduate or leave home. Equip me with appropriate boundaries for the older kids still at home. Thank you for always being with me in every aspect of parenting. Amen.

1. What are the challenges with your teens or young adults asserting independence?

2. Do you have any boomerang kids in your house? What are your frustrations? What can you do to move them to independence?

3. In what ways are you tempted to parent on autopilot?

4. What areas may need to be reassessed in your current stage with your teen or young adult children?

17

Cultivate Your Identity

Fear not, for I have redeemed you; I have called you by your name;
You are Mine.
—ISAIAH 43:1 NKJV

In my years of "mom-ing," I've been a basketball, tennis, cross-country, track, soccer, baseball, volleyball, band, choir, 4-H, college sports, theater, and missionary mom. I've made meals and baked goods for youth groups, sports teams, and fundraisers, and have helped with more science fair projects than I care to remember. I'm a girl mom and I'm a boy mom three times. I've been a stay-at-home mom, a working mom, and a graduate school mom. I've been a farmer's wife, teacher, counselor, writer. The list goes on.

I didn't realize how much these roles defined me until the roles started shifting. As I changed careers and my kids grew older, I realized my identity was tied to what I did, rather than centered on being the woman God created me to be. My identity was "stolen" from the proper place God intended.

Whether you're a working mom or a stay-at-home mom, your identity is likely closely tied to the title of "mom." A friend of mine recently said she had her identity crisis at forty when she realized how wrapped up she had been in being the parent of her three children. Another mom said she had her identity meltdown in her fifties, after her youngest graduated from college. My biggest identity crisis was in my midthirties when I went from being a stay-at-home mom to a working mom. Since then, what I think about myself is constantly readjusting when my professional or parenting roles change.

Do you have a case of stolen identity, in which the roles you fill rob you of your identity as a unique individual created by God? Most of us do. During the childrearing years, your parenting role easily becomes your identity. But it's not. Being a parent is something you *do*; it's a role you fill.

It's not who you are.

Moms of every generation have struggled with separating the role of motherhood from their identity. Before being a mom, you are first and foremost a daughter of the most high God. You are a woman made in the image of God for the purpose of glorifying him. Isaiah 43:7 says everyone was created by God for his glory, and that God calls you by name.

Unfortunately, girls are socialized from early childhood to believe that being a mother is the ultimate purpose in life. They are told motherhood is what will give them value and worth as adults. Be honest: When you first became a mom, did you feel as though you had somehow arrived?

Most moms I talk to have. Yet motherhood is only one role in your life as a woman of God.

God created women to be givers of life—not just physiologically, but through nurture, compassion, encouragement, and care. We are women first, created to be a life-giving presence to those around us for God's glory. This—not just physically giving birth— is God's call for all women. Not all women are moms, and that fact does not take away from their calling, value, or purpose.

We are life-givers to glorify Christ, no matter what stage of life. During the childrearing years, it's easy to focus so much on motherhood it becomes your only identity and your priorities get skewed. Let's look at the importance of identity outside of your role as mom.

YOU'RE NOT A MAID | In my book *Balance, Busyness, and Not Doing It All*, I write that the first priority for moms is to nurture; it's not to be the family's maid. Yet how much of your energy is spent on household chores: picking up after your kids, folding laundry, and preparing meals?

This may have been your primary role when your kids were young and unable to take care of their personal needs. You may even *enjoy* doing these tasks for your kids. But they do not constitute your identity. None of the roles you may take on—parent, spouse, child, employee, business owner, friend, volunteer—are your identity.

But being mom is what you *know*. You do it twenty-four hours a day for twenty or more years. Unfortunately, you don't get a lifetime achievement award recognizing your exemplary service when your kids leave home. Yet parenting has been your heart and soul.

In reality, your very being is sewed inside your kids, and they are unaware of it. So each child who becomes independent takes part of *you* with them, and they never even know it. If you don't cultivate *your* separate and autonomous identity, you'll be lost when the last one leaves home.

Let's distinguish *roles* from *identity*. Take a minute and, in the "Building up and letting go" section, write down all the roles you fill. For example, I'm a wife, mom, counselor, writer, speaker, life coach, daughter, and friend.

Write your list.

These are titles you *have*, complete with formal or informal job descriptions. When kids leave and these roles change, you may feel there's nothing left, but that's not true. You are a complete, whole person because you *are*. You are valuable and uniquely designed by the Father of creation. Psalm 139 says you were known by God even before the foundations of the world were established. The entire psalm gives an intimate picture of God's forethought and his knowledge of and plan for you. You, alone, are enough. Nothing added to you or taken from you will devalue your intrinsic worth in the eyes of God.

Unfortunately, you learn the unwritten societal rules. One of these rules is that being a mom makes you valuable. Raising "good kids" gives additional value. Add to that having a successful career, great husband, big house, attractive figure, well-behaved kids, nice clothes, fancy car—not to mention being a good cook, volunteer, and model Christian—and you've hit the jackpot. You're Wonder Woman! Super Mom! A great, fantastic person who has it all.

If you've been striving after those things to define you, you'll be disappointed when your kids mess up, when you lose your job, when the belly fat and premenopausal hormones take over, and when your kids walk out that door.

Super Mom isn't your identity. Mediocre Mom isn't either.

You're a daughter of the King. You are more than what you do or look like. You've been given the privilege of raising children who are also made for his glory. But you fulfill your calling as a woman of God when you use your life-giving gifts both in and outside of the family.

ACCEPTING YOURSELF | Do you feel uncomfortable thinking about who you are without your roles, titles, or accolades to hide behind? Thinking about yourself just as you are feels raw and vulnerable. There was a defining moment as a young mom when I felt raw and vulnerable before God, but he used my insecurities to change my perspective about myself.

Years ago, I was criticized by someone whom I looked up to. After putting the kids down for a nap, I curled up on our couch and cried out to God, asking him why he made me the way he did. I seemed to always mess up. I was pouring out to God what seemed like a lifetime of self-loathing when he gently reminded me he wasn't surprised by my weaknesses. In fact, God had made those parts of who I was, in balance with my strengths.

That moment was the first time I realized God made me a *whole* person, complete with the good, bad, and ugly; complete with strengths and weaknesses. Up to that point, I'd spent most of my life trying to fix myself. I find most women believe there's something inherently wrong with them. We spend much of our lives trying to create a more acceptable version of who we think we should be.

The truth is we are sinful people made in the image of an almighty God (Romans 3:23). God made us with natural strengths but also natural weaknesses. Yet, we strive to fix our weaknesses and downplay our strengths. We're taught to be humble, so we lack confidence to excel at what we do well. We work harder to change our weaknesses instead of putting that energy toward our strengths.

Does that sound crazy?

It is. Yet most of us do it. We spend our twenties trying to compensate for our childhood insecurities and then our thirties striving to be Superwoman. We arrive at midlife exhausted and in search of our real identities underneath those roles and titles.

Don't strive to be someone you think you *should* be. Accept yourself as God made you, strengths and weaknesses together. Receive the gift of being a *woman*, separate from your role as a mother. Women who are not mothers are not any less valuable than those of us who are. Unfortunately, the belief that motherhood is what gives a woman worth has existed in most cultures since the beginning of time. It's a damaging belief.

Being a mom is something you do; it's not who you *are*. When you accept this, you'll be more peaceful, confident, and free as each child walks out the door.

Stop the craziness of trying to be Super Mom. Avoid seeking your identity in performance-based activities. Feel comfortable with your strengths, weaknesses, and those quirky things about you. Release the perfect image and stop comparing yourself to Instagram Girl. Instead, look at the reflection God sees of you. To do so, follow these steps:

1. Go to the first question at the end of the chapter and take several minutes to list your strengths. Include things you love to do, things you do well, and the positive qualities about your natural temperament and personality. List every strength that makes you unique and special. Are

you a listener, encourager, or analyzer? Are you creative, a good cook, or a natural at math? Just start listing.

2. Now it's time to be honest about your "lesser strengths." We've referred to them as weaknesses so far, but Kenn Gividen refers to them as "lesser strengths" in his book *The Prayer of Hannah*. Focusing on them as weaknesses makes them something to loathe. Reframed as lesser strengths, these areas simply take a secondary role to your strengths.

   For example, I don't like to cook, but I do it every day. Cooking is a lesser strength. Rather than berate myself that I don't cook like my sister or spend hours trying to do it better, I just accept it and do the best I can. I'm also not the most patient person by nature. I've had to let God teach me patience so my impulsivity doesn't make a mess of situations. Second Corinthians 12:9 says, "My grace is sufficient for you, for my power is made perfect in weakness." Christ works in our weaknesses. When we acknowledge our lesser strengths, we can allow Christ's power to take over.

   On our own, our lesser strengths bear little fruit except insecurities, shame, and self-hatred. Accepting them and allowing God to work in them releases our priorities, time, and energy to be used for his glory. Accepting your lesser strengths reroutes your identity from being a mom, wife, or professional to simply being *you*.

   Take a moment now and list your lesser strengths in the section at the end of the chapter. Then release them to God.

3. Accept yourself as the whole person God made. Simply you. Simply enough.

PRACTICAL APPLICATION | What difference does this exercise make in your season of life?

Accepting yourself as you are fills the vacuum of an impending identity crisis. It prepares you for changing roles as your kids leave home. It empowers you to feel comfortable as your body, hormones, womanhood, and parenting roles change. Embracing your identity is one the greatest gifts you can receive. Grow your God-given strengths. Foster your passions which bring you joy, new opportunities, and fellowship with new friends.

Your strengths should be used in all areas of life. Your professional and personal roles continue to grow and change as your kids leave. Now, take your place of value as a woman of the almighty God.

BUILDING UP
and letting go

Father, thank you for creating me the way you did. Thank you for my strengths. Thank you also for my lesser strengths. Teach me to use all of them for your glory in my role as your daughter. Teach me contentment with who I am outside of being a mom. Amen.

1. Strengths: List your strengths (see text above for ideas).

2. Lesser strengths: List your lesser strengths. Then release them to God, allowing his strength to be made perfect in your weaknesses.

3. List all the roles you fill.

4. What are practical ways you can grow or use your gifts?

5. What principle can you apply right now?

18

Accept Midlife
with Grace

*Charm is deceptive, and beauty is fleeting, but a woman who fears
the Lord is to be praised. Honor her for all that her hands have
done, and let her works bring her praise at the city gate.*
—PROVERBS 31:30-31

I was browsing through the racks of infant clothes, longing for
the baby girl I still dreamed of having. At the time, Ethan was
two years old, and I could barely handle the four kids I had. Yet,
after having three boys, I wanted a little girl to be my youngest. I
thought a girl would stay around home in the final years of childrearing when the others were leaving. She'd be tied to my apron
strings, filling my needs during the last years of letting go, and my
parenting years would end in happiness and bliss.

She, the tagalong baby, would keep me young, healthy, and
vibrant. I wanted more kids for all the wrong reasons.

I'm now in my late forties, with three in their twenties and
one teenager. At times I still long to have younger kids coming up
through the ranks. Sometimes I envy peers who have tagalongs, or
who started their families later than we did.

It's yet another type of grief to be honest about: envying others who have what you're grieving. A full house, a youthful family, and a life you no longer have.

Facing midlife is different for each of us. Accepting it is critical to your growth as a woman and individual. However, the claim that "fifty is the new thirty" gives the illusion that age is relative. It's not. Here's reality. At forty-four, I ran a half marathon. It had been on my bucket list, and I felt unstoppable when I completed it. I thought I had this aging thing conquered. I believed if you just stay fit and healthy, things won't really change.

Three months after the half marathon, I played in a staff-student basketball game at the school where I worked when my knee gave out. I tore the meniscus and the ACL. I had major surgery and rehab and still have a permanently torn ACL in one of my knees.

So much for feeling on top of the world. Now I can't climb a staircase without limping.

The truth about aging? My kids say I'm hard of hearing (they really just mumble). I'm more tired. I have age spots and hair growing on my face I've never noticed before. I just ordered chains for my glasses because I forget where I put them. Usually they're just on my head.

Midlife is not young. But it's not old. It's a weird stage where everything you know is changing. It creeps up when you're not looking. You wake up to find your body isn't the same, your kids aren't the same, and your emotions aren't the same. With each child who graduates, your life isn't the same.

Some days, it stinks.

But it doesn't have to be that way. The more I embrace where I'm at and live it well, the more content, confident, and happier I am. Let's look at how to do it with grace.

WHO AM I? | Social media makes midlife seem as easy as an inspirational quote equipping women with confidence about age spots, belly flab, and sagging eyelids. Instagram bombards us with photos of younger women whom we used to be like. Meanwhile, our saggy, baggy skin tells us we're not one of them anymore.

Midlife *feels* weird. I cry when I don't expect it. I feel sad, anxious, or irritable and I don't know why. My husband thinks I'm cranky. It might be PMS. It might be perimenopause or the real thing. The average age of menopause onset is fifty-one. But who has time to figure it out? We're too busy raising kids and dealing with *their* crankiness, tears, and fears. You don't have time for your own.

Confidence wanes in midlife because the thing you know most about—being a mom—is changing. Cooking for hordes of teenagers, washing baseball pants, and falling asleep to noisy girls in your daughter's bedroom: that's the stuff you *know*. This new stuff of adult kids, a revolving door, easy weight gain, and looking like your mom? This stuff is strange. It doesn't feel good.

Midlife crisis. The emptying nest. They're real. The first step to accepting midlife is to stop fighting it. Just be right where you are.

ACCEPTING GRACE | It was March in the Midwest, which meant I had been more sedentary and had eaten comfort food during the winter months. I felt old, and the clothes in my closet were too tight. I decided it was time to get clothes I felt comfortable and confident in at fortysomething. The decision wasn't just about weight; it was about accepting the new stage of midlife.

As a woman with a history of an eating disorder, this was an important moment. Instead of feeling insecure and loathing myself for not being the younger me, I gave myself permission to accept who I was now.

I was giving myself grace. In 2 Corinthians 12:9, Paul writes that the Lord told him, "My grace is sufficient for you, for my power is made perfect in weakness." I was choosing God's strength in my weakness—his grace to not fixate over diets or try to be the size I used to be. Grace to accept the face in the mirror that looks different than it used to. Grace to be who I am, not something I used to be, or should be, or want to be for the wrong reasons. Grace meant I really was okay with how I looked, but I needed a wardrobe that mirrored that too.

I wanted to be comfortable and confident with where I was now. I went to a local resale shop and found clothes that made me feel great in my fortysomething skin. It was the first step in accepting midlife and embracing a season I am still getting used to.

It's something you can do too.

UNDESERVED KINDNESS | Why is it that we, as women, are our worst enemies? In a culture that's increasingly about status, likes, followers, and staged photos, we are inundated with pressures to perform, succeed, and be the ideal even in the privacy of our own homes. We silently try to outdo one another.

That's just crazy. Our real lives aren't all put together!

A few years ago I did a #30DaysofReal series on Facebook, in which I posted unstaged photos taken around our home for thirty days. I wanted to encourage real life, faith, and parenting beyond the storybook image. Readers said, "Thank you! It's so nice to know my house isn't the only one that way!" and "It feels good to know I'm not alone because things aren't perfect at my house."

Being real with each other is important. Not just about our messy houses, but also about our messy lives.

By your midforties, much of what we've talked about has likely touched you or your family. You probably have wounds and scars, and your faith might even be challenged. It's hard to be honest about these things when everyone around you seems perfect. But accepting your imperfections makes you more confident when you don't have everything together, because you know others don't, either. It's freeing when you don't take yourself so seriously.

During graduate school, when I was a counselor in training, we were pushed to identify our weaknesses so they would not become stumbling blocks for future clients. Though the experience was painful, it led me to the cross of Jesus Christ. There, I received *his* acceptance and grace for my weaknesses and flaws. I didn't have to hide anything from him. I learned my worth in him was the same as it had been before the experience. I gained courage and freedom to accept myself as I am. Flawed. Capable of sin. Capable of love. Redeemed through God's grace.

God's grace is free. It can't be earned, which goes against the world's standards of performing, earning, and striving. It's humbling to receive it. But when you do, it's easier to extend it to others.

Grace is the greatest strategy for facing midlife. Being *here* is a pivotal moment. You ponder life—where you've been, where you are, and where you want to be. I'd challenge the idea that midlife is a *crisis*. You're not in crisis; you're in a big life transition. Multiple things in this season are changing—your family, your body, and your roles. There is only one thing that remains constant through all the changes—Jesus Christ. Several passages in the Bible talk about God's unchanging character.

Malachi 3:6 says, "I the Lord do not change."

Hebrews 13:8 says, "Jesus Christ is the same yesterday and today and forever."

James 1:17 says, "Every good and perfect gift is from above, coming down from the Father of the heavenly lights, who does not change like shifting shadows."

Jesus' love, forgiveness, and grace never change though everything around you is.

REAL GUILT VERSUS FALSE GUILT | A lot of midlifers reflect and look back on life. You see where you could have done things differently, where you've failed or where your kids have screwed up. You may feel guilty for the pain or outcomes in your family or your child's life. There are a lot of "what ifs" and "if onlys": If only I would have known . . . What if I would have done this differently . . . If only I would have responded by . . .

You may feel guilty for hurts you've caused. Our feel-good culture is so accustomed to making us feel good in our mess that it's not popular to talk about guilt. But it's necessary. You may need to deal with guilt and consequences from your choices. It's important, however, to distinguish real guilt from false guilt.

Real guilt. Real guilt is what you *should* feel when you've sinned against Christ or another person and when you have done something harmful toward another individual. This guilt should result in change, responsibility, repentance, and restitution. When

I was guilty for allowing my anger to affect our family, I needed to change. I had to be responsible for it, ask for forgiveness, and make things right. Ignoring it or excusing it without changing it would have been wrong. I had real guilt.

If you are aware of behavior or choices of yours which have directly harmed your child or family and you haven't addressed it, do so. Make changes, work at the relationships, give up control, and ask for forgiveness. If your teen or young adult needs professional help because of it, get the services needed.

Then receive Christ's forgiveness and grace and walk forward.

False guilt. On the other hand, false guilt is what you or others impose on you for things for which you are not responsible. If your child is making poor choices because of hurt you've caused her, once you've taken appropriate responsibility for it, you cannot be continually blamed and shamed for her actions. She, too, has to take responsibility for her behavior. People emotionally manipulate with false guilt by blaming others.

False guilt is not godly conviction. God creates each of us with choice and responsibility for our actions, attitudes, and words. Teens, young adults, and adults are responsible for their behavior. Romans 14:12 says, "So then, each of us will give an account of ourselves to God." The Bible also says, "If we confess our sins, he is faithful and just and will forgive us our sins and purify us from all unrighteousness" (1 John 1:9).

God's grace is complete and balanced. He expects responsibility and is generous with forgiveness and grace. It's why I love him so much.

You can spend midlife chastising yourself for your regrets and do-overs, but it's a waste of time. Take care of what needs to be taken care of, bring it to the cross of Jesus, and then receive Jesus' grace. In turn, model Christ to your kids. Expect responsibility but also extend forgiveness and grace.

Your kids and mine will mess up. Our responsibility is to have a godly response that doesn't enable, excuse, or embrace either legalism or cheap grace. We are to respond with humility, empathy, accountability, and mercy.

WHAT IT LOOKS LIKE | How do you practically extend grace to yourself and walk humbly with your children, no matter their ages?

- Tell yourself that you parented the best you knew how at the time.
- Trust that God is bigger than your failures.
- Pray prayers of praise, thanksgiving, and intercession.
- Have faith that Christ will work in your children's lives despite *their* choices or *your* failures.
- Focus on what needs to change for you or your child to be healthy.
- Don't worry about what other people think.
- Obey what God's asking *you* to do for the health and safety of your family.

Guilt could have paralyzed me when I finally saw how my behavior affected my kids and marriage. However, all I could do was confess my sin, ask for forgiveness, and change unhealthy behavior. I had to leave the results to God.

As children of the heavenly Father, we have hope that Jesus is bigger than our failures. He *does* redeem the years. As Lamentations 3:22-23 says, his mercies *are* new every morning.

No one else is raising your child or parenting your young adult but you. Some will misjudge you or your family. Some will blame you for your child's choices. The truth is that each of us is responsible for our behavior—you for yours and your children for theirs.

At midlife, we still have years ahead of us to create our legacy. Creating a godly heritage requires standing firm in God's truth and moving forward in his grace.

BUILDING UP
and letting go

Lord, thank you for this season of life. Thank you for the fullness of your grace that goes beyond any of my sins and failures. Equip me to know your grace and to extend grace to myself and others, especially my kids. Thank you for your Son, Jesus Christ, the author and perfecter of grace. Amen.

1. What are your honest struggles with reaching midlife?

2. What truths about do-overs do you need to embrace and to begin living?

3. What areas do you need to honestly confess before God and, if needed, your children? How do you change them?

4. In what areas do you need to extend to yourself grace?

19

Friendships and Loneliness

Two are better than one, because they have a good return for their labor:
  If either of them falls down, one can help the other up.
—ECCLESIASTES 4:9-10

"I desire friendship," I wrote in my journal. Tears ran down my cheeks as I shared my thoughts with God. I felt stupid. What a selfish thing to write, I thought. I have friends.

Well . . . I mean, I *had* friends—before life got busy. Before I was needed at every turn. Before sleep became my preferred activity after a long day of work, running kids around, and everything in between.

What I had now were *relationships*. Work relationships. Church relationships. Facebook and Instagram relationships. Relationships with other moms with whom I used to be close friends and to whom now I just said hi at school events. I had plenty of people around me, many of whom would call me their friend. What was my problem?

I realized I was missing something.

I missed calling a friend or two for a playdate because I needed companionship and they had time. I missed our families hanging out on weekends, sometimes with more than twenty kids between us, laughing and talking about mom stuff. That was before ball games, chauffeuring, checking in with my parents, and managing my kids' schedules overtook my calendar.

I still had friends, but we weren't present in each other's lives in the same way. And it felt lonely.

But I also realized relationships had appropriately shifted for this season. I'm investing in my family with the limited time and energy I have before they're gone, and my friends are too.

Like listening to the college kid who calls you, crying and homesick, while you're cleaning up the fifth-grader's science fair project that he waited until the last minute to do. The junior high kid is yelling, "Where's the toothpaste?" and the high schooler is in his room, behind a locked door, ignoring everyone.

These are the people around me all the time, and I can barely keep up with them. I feel as though I have no friends because I'm doing the best I can with *these* people who are right in front of me.

Sound familiar? Let's talk about this loneliness stuff and how to stay connected with friends during this disconnected season.

WHERE DID EVERYONE GO? | "When you try to make plans with your mom friends and realize none of you are free for the next twenty years": this was a Facebook meme posted by a friend when her firstborn was a high school senior. It's so true. We are all so busy raising our families that maintaining friendships is a challenge. It's difficult to know how to hold on to old relationships and build new ones while still engaging with your family.

During these hectic years, your friends often consist of parents from your kids' sports teams and activities. But those friendships change when your kids graduate or change activities. Many of our parent-friends who had kids Jenna's and Mark's ages are now empty nesters or grandparents. Our paths don't cross the way they did when our kids were in school together. They are busy traveling or playing with grandkids, and I'm still making team meals and cleaning up after fundraisers. We see each other at our kids' weddings, where we laugh and cry at the memories of our kids growing up.

Then there are the younger parent-friends of Drew's and Ethan's peers. Many are in the "full house" years, without any children yet in college. They volunteer and attend a lot of their kids' events. They still look put together and haven't entered the frazzled, weird, emotional zone yet. I'm the seasoned mom who feels like a misfit because I'm on top of things for one kid, but for another one, not so much.

Like when the eighth-grade graduation ceremony crept up on us and I realized Ethan needed to wear a tie and dress shirt. As the youngest of three boys, he has a closet full of hand-me-down clothes, and I never thought about buying him something new or asking him what he wanted to wear. So, the night the before the ceremony, I picked out a white dress shirt, a tie of his dad's, and khaki pants. He was good to go. I'd done this three times before, right? Not a problem.

But the old mom didn't get the memo that white shirts, dress ties, and khaki pants were out. I didn't think to ask if Ethan wanted to shop for his event. I honestly gave no thought about what he would wear other than what I'd picked out. To me it was another busy day, just another milestone I had done before. I at least made sure I got off work for the graduation ceremony.

Jenna and Mark were coming home from college that weekend, and I was busy planning the revolving-door schedule of who would be in and out of our house for the summer.

When I found my seat in the auditorium, I relaxed for a few minutes only to be mortified at my hand-me-down kid wearing a white shirt, khaki pants, and dress tie amid the sea of young men in hip, bright colors with bow ties and black pants. It was a mom fail of significant proportion. I wanted to laugh and cry all at the same time. I had major midlife mom grief and no one in my life stage to share it with.

This emptying nest is not just our kids leaving, it's a personal emptiness too. You are busy with family, career, and caring for your own parents as they age. Kids are the common denominator in many friendships. Some of your old friends move on, relocate, or have different interests or values.

And it's lonely.

I wrote a blogpost titled "I Have No Friends and Other Mom Grief." It brought a big response from midlife and empty-nest women who expressed mutual loneliness and grief. The struggle is real. Being with your kids, building your career, investing in your marriage, caring for aging parents, and trying to do self-care— when do you possibly have time for friends?

And when do they possibly have time for you?

THE FRIENDS WHO ARE | The friends you may find time for in this season are often the ones you reach out to when the storms come—one of you has a failing marriage, a rebellious teen, or a young adult with an addiction. These are the friends you listen to, cry with, and pray for without judging them or their kids. Because they do the same for you.

These are the friends to whom you can say, "This wasn't supposed to be my life."

These friendships don't just happen; they're cultivated. As your families and lifestyles change, you pursue these friends because you value them, and they value you.

I'm walking in hard places with some of these friends right now, as they have walked with me. If you have one safe person you can call when your world is crumbling down, it's a gift.

And the other friends? You'll have fun times with them again, or you'll develop new friendships with people who have common interests in a post-kid life. When my parents were empty nesters, they started traveling, and they seemed to be doing things with friends all the time. I remember wondering, "What happened to my parents? They don't travel. And who are these friends I don't know about?"

My parents finally had time to do things with others and didn't have to check in with anyone. It's something to look forward to!

But for a few more years, we need to spend time with our kids. Social things will happen again. For now, evenings and weekends and family vacations with my kids are times I cherish. My kids fill most of the space that friends used to fill, and that's okay.

RECONNECTING AND INVESTING | Realistically, though, you do need people in your life other than your kids. Those mom-grief moments are real, and only women can understand what you're going through. Your kids fill up your time, but they don't take the place of mutual friendships. Many of you are also caring for aging parents, and those relationships are draining. You and I need each other. So how do we reconnect with friends in the limited time we have? What relationships should take priority?

- Assess your loneliness and friendship grief. Is there a particular person you miss in your life? If so, why have you grown apart? If you miss the friendship, try to reconnect with that person. Ask her out for coffee. Go to a movie. Just reach out. I recently did this with someone with whom I'd grown apart over the last few years. We both had new jobs, her kids were married, and she and her husband travel a lot. We were able to spend a weekend together, and we picked up right where we left off years ago. We laughed, cried, and were glad for the time together.
- Go beyond being online friends. Social media is a great place to connect with people. I'd encourage you, however, to get beyond just being Facebook friends. Connect with them in real life. Make a phone call or get together in person to have meaningful conversations.
- Assess relationships. Some friendships may not be healthy. If a friendship is draining you or causing stress, it's okay to set appropriate boundaries with that friend. If a former friend is toxic, be kind to them, but you don't need to pursue that relationship.

- Invest in your marriage before the kids leave. The upcoming transition might be harder than you think (more on this in the next chapter!).
- Invest in the only relationship that brings true fulfillment: a personal relationship with Jesus Christ. If you aren't in the habit of having a personal devotional time, set aside a few times a week to do so. All you need is a Bible and perhaps a journal. Spend fifteen minutes in a quiet place where you can read Scripture and pray, bringing all of your needs before God. Use a Bible app on your phone and read while waiting in the carpool line or for a ball game to start. If you've never journaled, you can write, draw, or doodle while you read Scripture and pray. There are many types of Scripture or prayer journals available to connect with your personal style. Ultimately, before you look to others to fill some of the longings in your heart, take care of the most important relationship: the one with your heavenly Father (Matthew 22:37). As the kids leave, time for this relationship does open up!

ASSESSING YOUR NEEDS AND BUILDING COMMUNITY | The longing for connection is also met through people with whom you can build new friendships through activities and common interests. Many women abandon hobbies during the full-house years. Your interests can change between the time you're a young mom and the time your kids are older. In the process of cultivating your identity, invest in activities that connect you with people who share similar interests. I have writer friends, speaker friends, and ministry friends. These relationships are different than those with my church or "bleacher mom" friends, but they are valuable because they connect with the "me" outside of home and family.

Look for new peer groups in your community outside of your kids' school. Attend a community Bible study or exercise class, or volunteer in an area of your passion. Start a book club for people in a similar stage of life. A friend of mine started a group specifically for women in their forties and fifties who are at this transitional season. Use this book for a small group study or as a conversation starter!

Even though we're connected more than ever through technology, we still need real people with whom we can laugh, cry, and pray. Seek them out. Build a community with the relationships God has placed around you.

BUILDING UP
and letting go

Father, thank you for the gift of friendships, even though at this phase of life they are different from what they used to be. Help me to reach out and connect with those around me so I can also be an encouragement to them. Sustain me in the times I feel alone. Thank you that I am truly not ever alone, because you are with me. Amen.

1. Take a few minutes to assess your needs for community and relationships. What are your longings?

2. What friendships are your treasures in this season? Are there friends with whom you'd like to reconnect?

3. Are there relationships that you need to sever because they are toxic or damaging?

4. Where can you reach out to build community for your needs?

20

Love, Marriage, and Mom and Dad

You are precious and honored in my sight,
*   and . . . I love you.*
—ISAIAH 43:4

Ron and I sat together awkwardly in the living room that Sunday evening. It was our first time home by ourselves after Drew and Mark left for college and Jenna moved to Mexico. Ethan was our sole child left to dote on, and he was with the youth group, spending time at an area homeless shelter.

We looked at the clock and wondered when Ethan would get home. We had been expecting that he would be home by then. We watched TV, but the family room was painfully quiet.

"We're pathetic," Ron said, as we talked back and forth about whether we should text Ethan to see where he was.

"I miss my kids," I simply said.

While I should have been embracing the time with just Ron, I wasn't quite ready for the *him and me* time yet. I know I shouldn't have felt that way, but I did. It had been more than twenty-five years since he and I had a lot of time alone together, and it was going to take some getting used to.

Navigating the nonchild relationships in your life is another midlife challenge. Ron and I have had several discussions about this new experience of togetherness. We have different expectations, and we've had to be frank with each other about what we need as we ease into more time with just the two of us.

While your kids may not need you as much, others do. Your spouse. Aging parents. You take your eyes off your kids, and others are there waiting for your time, attention, and nurture. Honestly, if you're like me, you may need some physical and emotional space in this huge transition. The adjustment for you, the nurturer, is something your spouse or others may not understand. Your kids have been your primary focus for twenty or so years. You might not be fully ready to care for others in their place. It's important to be honest with yourself and others.

YOUR MARRIAGE: SURVIVING AND THRIVING | "Today's our twenty-fifth wedding anniversary!" I told the office staff at my workplace when the florist delivered flowers. Our kids had sent them to me to celebrate our big milestone (which, to be honest, had crept up on me).

"My twenty-fifth anniversary was the year I left my husband," a colleague said.

The awkward response hung in the air. I smiled and took my flowers to my office. Then I thought about how many marriages around me hadn't made it to twenty-five years. Of the eight of us in the office that day, there were only three of us who weren't divorced.

Raising kids can be rough on a marriage. Spouses focus on children and careers when kids are young. Before you know it, you don't talk about anything other than your kids. As those kids start leaving the nest, you feel as though you no longer know the person you married. And during those eighteen to twenty years, both of you have changed.

I remembered the day my college roommate called me to say her mom and dad were getting a divorce. It was the week after my friend had announced her engagement. She was the youngest child and was the apple of her dad's eye. It appeared that since his daughter was getting married, there was no reason for him to stay married anymore.

If you've encountered any of the hard situations we've talked about so far, you're familiar with the stress that struggling teens or young adults have on a marriage. When there is stress and chaos in your home, just staying afloat takes the energy you would otherwise put toward your marriage. Doing more than that is too exhausting.

But even healthy marriages can struggle when kids leave because you and your spouse may handle these experiences differently. Your husband may be ready for the kids to leave, whereas you're wrestling with mom grief. My husband and I are still working on this process of differing expectations and needs without kids around all the time. I still need my space. I need him to not hover. And he needs things too.

We *do* have different needs. Some days, I physically miss my kids not being at home. Being alone with my spouse reminds me even more of the changes in our family. Working through these changes have been essential for us during this phase. It's easy to misperceive each other's responses or to have expectations that the other person can't meet. When the gap between us seems too big, I often simply say, "We're on the same team."

That's how it is for us, but each couple is different. In your marriage it may be the other way around. You might crave time to finally be with your husband, and he might need space to process the changes in family, midlife, and identity. These things happen in his world too.

On top of raising a family, marriage itself can be hard. As a therapist, I have worked with many couples in complicated, difficult, and even toxic marriages. A lot of Christian marriages struggle with really tough issues. I can't talk about marriage without being honest about a few topics.

First, God intended marriages to last a lifetime. Marriage is meant to be a permanent joining of two souls—a union that reflects God's eternal love for humanity. However, Christian marriages are not immune from divorce. This discussion is not intended to shame you if you are divorced or a single parent, or to persuade you to stay in a marriage that is abusive. The purpose of this section is to talk honestly to those who are married during these years and to discuss how to strengthen this relationship so the empty-nest years don't leave you ripe for a breakup.

In the simplest of terms, how do you foster your marriage relationship during this season of fledging kids from your nest? Here are a few principles:

- Be honest about where you are. I had to be honest with my husband about my need for personal space the first few months we were alone more often. I didn't want to push him away, but I needed alone time.
- Talk about what you want the empty-nest years to look like. We've had honest discussions about what we want to do when then kids are all gone. Traveling, hiking, and just hanging out are things we both look forward to. Looking ahead at those goals has helped me focus on what is ahead of us while we still have kids at home.
- Invest in your marriage. Date nights, walks, conversations about things other than kids are important through this season when kids are both in and out of the house.
- Invest in your future. Real problems can attack your marriage during these years. Sometimes the present tells you being married isn't worth the current pain. However, looking ahead to what marriage means after kids leave may give you a different perspective. Enjoying grandkids, seeing your adult children grow, cherishing companionship, and growing old together are the blessings of marriage after kids. Looking ahead helped me through some rough years when I could only see right in front of me. I've also seen many marriages at their worst during the parenting years and at their best in the years after.

- Give each other space to readjust. Your kids are an integral part of each of your lives. Give your spouse room to readjust to the changing roles and family, and give yourself room too. Don't expect your spouse to understand your mom grief or to adjust to the changes at the same pace you do. Give grace to each other as you adapt to your changing family.
- Focus on the things you have in common rather than your differences. Many marriages break up after the kids leave because spouses don't feel that they know each other. Marriages that primarily focus on kids during the parenting years are most vulnerable for breakup after they go. If you find yourself estranged from your spouse because you've lived parallel lives around your kids, focus on the things you have in common—your kids, your past, your future. As you grow and develop as individuals, you won't be the exact person you were decades earlier. Instead of letting that divide your marriage, find new ways to connect. Get to know the new interests of your spouse and reconnect with the things you enjoyed before kids.
- Seek professional help when needed. Counseling is critical for many of the issues facing marriages and families during these years. Don't wait for counseling to be your last resort to save a marriage. Seek counsel to help you with things you can't do on your own. Whether you do it as a couple or individually, be proactive rather than reactive about outside support. Kids themselves can tear apart parents' marriages, along with toxic behavior, mental health issues, addiction, grief over a child's death, enabling, enmeshment, or codependency. Enlisting professional help during stressful family situations guards the health of your marriage and family.
- Be realistic about the state of your relationship. Emotionally damaging or abusive relationships (mentally, emotionally, sexually, or physically) are exceptions to the suggestions above. If your marriage is toxic because your spouse is abusive, be honest with yourself and others. Seek support from agencies, therapists, or resources that assist in these

situations.[1] Abuse is *never* okay. God cares about *you* and
your health and safety.

- Invest in *you*. Apply the principles in the chapters on identity, self-care, and giving yourself grace.

WHEN YOUR KIDS MARRY | "This is how it's supposed to be,"
I told myself as Samantha helped Mark unpack his clothes and put
them in his dorm room when we moved him in as a college freshman. It was the first time I really realized that, as his girlfriend,
Samantha had a place in Mark's heart that was no longer mine.
Even though he and Samantha were not yet engaged or married
and Samantha was still a high school senior, their love for each
other was undeniable. We already knew she was the one for him.
In many ways, this day of saying goodbye really belonged to the
two of them, not to me and my son. Watching how hard it was for
him to say goodbye to her was my cue to a big lesson: that letting
go means releasing your kids to their future spouses too.

I was reminded of Matthew 19:5: "Therefore a man shall leave
his father and his mother and hold fast to his wife, and the two
shall become one flesh" (ESV). As Ron and I have walked with
Mark and Samantha through their engagement and recent marriage, I have been reminded that godly parenting means aiming
my kids toward the spouse they love and to whom they will hold
fast. The one who came from my womb now is one flesh with his
partner through marriage.

It's another transition, another experience to work through.
Here are a few thoughts about adult kids, relationships, and marriage. (Note: These suggestions are for adult relationships, not
teen relationships. Those require another chapter, perhaps even
another book!)

- Your young adults need autonomy in their relationships. Step
  back and let them figure things out. This can be hard, especially if you think their dating relationships aren't healthy, or

---

1. Author Leslie Vernick has resources for those who have experienced emotionally
damaging relationships. Also, seek out your local domestic violence agency or the
National Domestic Violence Hotline: 1-800-799-7233 or www.thehotline.org.

if the person your young adult has chosen wouldn't be your first choice for a dating or marriage partner. Regardless of these questions, you can still invest in *your* relationship with your child. Instead of telling her what you don't like about the person or forcing her to choose between you and her partner, keep your mind and heart open. Be approachable so you can give insight and counsel, but step back from dictating whom your child should or shouldn't date or marry. Exceptions are mentioned below.

- Don't pressure your young adult to marry too quickly. "Get a ring by spring" is the unwritten message at a lot of Christian colleges, which puts pressure on kids to marry for the sake of taking the traditional "next step." Young adults should take their time finding the right person. Kids are growing up with a fantasy view of marriage because of social media and reality TV shows that glamorize weddings and idealize relationships. *Marriage* is not the goal for adulthood; being a healthy adult is. Don't pressure your young adult toward marriage just because you think he is the right age for it or because you think he might not find a partner later on.

- Let go when your children marry. Your children need to focus on their spouses. You are there for support, but they need to figure out their life together apart from you.

- There are always exceptions. In cases of abusive relationships—whether the abuse is emotional, sexual, mental, or physical—your role is to support and help your child. If your young adult shows signs of abuse of any kind while dating, reach out to support her. Talk about healthy relationships and boundaries. Develop a safety plan. The same is true if your adult child is in a marriage relationship, although it's more difficult because of the legal conditions binding the marriage or any children who may be in the picture. Advocate for your child and make yourself available so your son or daughter knows you are safe to reach out to. Seek out local or national agencies—for example, the National Domestic Violence Hotline—for how to support or help any children who are in abusive relationships. Let them know, no matter what, that you believe them and have their back.

- Invest in your relationship with your adult child and any significant other or spouse. Don't fight or be controlling about little things. If your young adult is in a sexual relationship outside of marriage or in a relationship you don't approve of, keep the lines of communication open. Let your young person know you value him as a person outside of his lifestyle or relationship choices. Relationship parenting is your lifetime investment.

TAKING CARE OF MOM AND DAD | Your adult kids need you less, your spouse needs you in different ways, and your own parents may need you more. There are real reasons why you feel like you're crazy some days!

Being in the so-called sandwich generation is exhausting: you may be parenting minors, adult children, and elderly parents all at the same time. You may even have grandchildren, too. Some people refer to this as the "panini generation," because you're pushed, squeezed, and heated up on all sides! If you find yourself being a caregiver to your own parents or parents-in-law during the releasing years, here are a few words of encouragement:

- Many principles that apply to your kids about enabling, boundaries, and enmeshment also apply to your aging parents. If you are doing things for elderly parents they are able to do themselves, it's okay to draw boundaries, even though they may fuss. There are certain things only you can do, but there are things they can do for themselves. When that's the case, let them do it.
- Speak up about your caregiving needs with siblings, your spouse, and even your kids. Unless you are an only child carrying the needs of an aging parent, advocate for your needs with your siblings or your other parent. Set healthy boundaries. Don't be a caregiver alone.
- Practice self-care. Repeat.

- Balance the needs of your parent with the needs of the kids you're still raising. Enlist other care providers when needed so you can spend time with the kids you still have at home.
- Don't take on false guilt from a parent, siblings, or others. Remember, false guilt is what others impose on you to manipulate you or make you feel bad for something for which you are not responsible.
- Give yourself grace. Repeat daily if needed.
- You can't do everything—so don't.
- Seek a support group for caregivers or seek out a friend with whom you can share your honest feelings, and rest.
- Pray. Repeat.

These different relationships are all part of this stage of life. This is an annotated version of the topics, and I've included an appendix with suggestions for parents of kids with special needs. If you need more resources in these areas, there are specialized books and resources for each of them.

Take care of yourself and give yourself grace in this season, knowing how much God loves *you* as you pour yourself out to others.

BUILDING UP
and letting go

Father, thank you for these relationships—my parents, spouse, and children. Help me to do what I can to foster healthy relationships in each area. Thank you for your grace when I need it, and for your discernment when I need to reach out for help. Thank you for caring about me. Amen.

1. What are the biggest struggles in your marriage right now? What can you do to improve your marriage relationship?

2. What has challenged you about letting go of your kids and their romantic relationships?

3. How can you take care of yourself if you're a caregiver for your parents?

4. What is one principle that encouraged or challenged you?

21

Don't Miss this Life

He makes me lie down in green pastures, he leads me beside quiet waters, he refreshes my soul.
—PSALM 23:1-3

We were watching Drew play a college basketball game at one of the universities where I attended graduate school. It had been eight years since I first set foot on that campus. Life had changed so much since then. The life path I thought I was pursuing turned out to be different than the one I had anticipated. At age forty, I had left a teaching career for graduate school. My kids were in second, fifth, eighth, and eleventh grade at the time.

So much has happened since then. In those eight years, I completed a master's degree and two licensure programs from two different universities, completing a dual internship of 1,600 hours. I have been a school counselor and a private therapist, and have become licensed in my field. I've also become an author and speaker, teaching at conferences and retreats on women's issues, mental health, parenting, writing, and faith.

I've been to four state championships with my child athletes, have seen my daughter live in two other countries, and have a son who received a full-ride scholarship. I now watch one son play the sport he loves at the collegiate level.

I've celebrated twenty-eight years of marriage and am still raising a teenager.

Even after these "successes," I still wonder if I should be producing or volunteering more or getting involved in something that I'm not. When I look at what others are doing, I sometimes feel I'm not doing enough. Maybe you do too.

Where do we get that crazy idea that we aren't doing enough? I don't share these accomplishments to say what great things I've done, because I'm surrounded by amazing women who also do a lot. I share because I'm alarmed at my own self-talk, and because I know others tell themselves these things too. The self-doubt that says you're not doing enough is not from God. It's from his adversary, who wants us distracted by accomplishing and doing more rather than simply following where God leads.

Eight years ago, I left teaching and prayed to find a part-time or flexible job in my skill set that would fit our family life before the kids all left home. God has answered all those prayers by providing new career options that complement our family during this season of life. I didn't set out to be a speaker or published author. I simply started writing from my own mess, wondering if others were struggling, too. I've tried to be obedient with a message of authentic hope.

On the outside, some may think I'm too busy. Others may think I'm not striving enough. But I'm right where I'm supposed to be, having mental and emotional space for my kids and husband. I have more peace than I've had in the last fifteen years by learning when to say yes and when to say no, when to say "Why not?" and when to say "Not now."

Being obedient to Christ is risky. It doesn't always fit in a predictable plan or traditional package onlookers understand. But his ways are better than our ways. I've learned life is not a race. At the end of our lives, people will miss *us*, not our accomplishments. They will remember who we invested in rather than what we did.

THE MOST IMPORTANT THREE WORDS | There's a 1970s folk song that tells the story of a dad and his son. The young dad tells his baby about things they're going to do as he gets bigger. Then the son is ten and the dad says he'll play when he gets back from a business trip. Soon the son is in college and is too busy for Dad. The son is even busier when he's a father.

The moral of the story is the heart of this book. The fledging season is probably the busiest season of your life. School activities, work responsibilities, weddings, graduations, caring for parents, and other big events. Life doesn't slow down, but it's also not a race.

We live our priorities in the daily activities while our kids grow up. We think there will be more time when the kids are older or when life slows down. But before you know it, they're out the door and the cycle continues. If you don't stop striving and embrace *now*, you'll miss the time that's right in front of you: Time to listen to your kid. Time to just hang out with your family. Time to say no to activities that can be done later in life when your kids are no longer at home.

The ways that parents prioritize family life and manage their time fall along a spectrum. One extreme is excessive busyness, in which parents chase after success or priorities that take them away from their kids. Most of us have done this at some point in time. Perhaps that describes you right now.

The other extreme is putting everything outside of parenting on hold until your kids are grown. You focus exclusively on your kids without investing in your marriage, other relationships, personal development, career, or your relationship with God. Parenting can be an idol when you put your kids above all other things, especially God.

Do you fall into either extreme? Are your priorities out of sync? Are you so busy you're missing what's in front of you? Or is your kids' happiness so central in your mind that you have no energy left for your marriage, vocation, church, or other involvements?

Ethan taught me a big lesson when he was in sixth grade. I was typing a blogpost when he came to me with a homework project he had been working on. "Are you busy?" he asked.

He was holding a board game on Andrew Carnegie that he had made for social studies. I cringed inside. Playing games is one of my least favorite mom tasks. But I knew that when a preteen or teen asks you if you're busy, it means he needs time with you. I also knew these were my last moments of playing board games with sixth-grade boys.

I told Ethan I'd love to play the game.

It took us only ten minutes.

In ten minutes, I heard what Ethan learned about Andrew Carnegie. I affirmed his creativity in the design of the game. When we were done, Ethan said, "Thanks, Mom," and gave me a huge grin. He packed up the game, went up to his room, and I finished writing.

Ten minutes meant nothing to my readers, but it meant the world to my son.

It means the world to your kids too.

When your child, teen, or young adult asks, "Are you busy?" pay attention. There's something important she needs from you. Those interrupted moments won't always be ten minutes for minor things. It might be half an hour, when your teen lets you into her world. Or an hour, when your college student calls because he needs reassurance. Or an afternoon, when your adult child tells you she really isn't okay.

Many students have told me they are afraid to talk to their parents about things going on in their lives. When asked why, they often say it's because Mom and Dad are too busy.

Our busyness speaks to our kids about priorities and whether they feel seen, known, or valued.

Teens, especially, are skeptical to share with their parents. When they do reach out, they do so cautiously. They likely won't start a formal conversation with, "There's something really important going on in my life, and I need to discuss it with you."

When they say, "Are you busy?" they're seeing if they are important enough to you for you to put down what you're doing to see and hear them. This is when you need to be less distracted so you can hear what's really going on in their world. There's a brief window for you to either connect with them or put them off. When your answer is that you're too busy, they eventually stop asking.

But you and I can't stop everything, right? There's work to do, bills to pay, and Facebook to check!

Really: it's about aligning priorities rather than dropping everything when a child asks. The challenge of parenting kids at various stages is assessing what needs to be done now, what can wait, and who needs you the most, all while keeping your sanity.

When I was teaching, my method of self-care was running. I ran two miles every day, rain or shine. As a working mom with four kids from toddler to middle school, I thought I had everything balanced. Our house ran smoothly; I took care of myself; things were great!

But something wasn't right, and one of the kids saw it. One of them saw that, while I thought I was doing it all, and doing it well, I was invested in things that took my time and attention away from them. They told me so one day . . . by hiding my running shoes.

To be honest, I was pouring a lot of time and attention into my lesson plans, my students, and myself at that time. Running had become an idol to me, and the Holy Spirit had been convicting me of it. But I had been pushing it off and ignoring it. Working moms are supposed to do it all.

But God wouldn't let me run from him. I still don't know which kid was the culprit, but one of them hid my running shoes in a very strategic, hard-to-find place. No one fessed up, but they didn't need to. God got my attention.

It's a lesson I'll never forget.

BALANCING PRIORITIES | Living a balanced life is about doing what's most important in the season you're living. It takes consistent intentional assessment.

So how do you practically determine what's best for your family and personal priorities? Here are a few key principles:

- Pray. Seek the Holy Spirit for wisdom about priorities in your parenting season. Priorities shift as your family changes. You don't have to be involved in everything right now. Ask God where you should be spending your time between work, family, and other activities. There's a time to say yes and a time to say no. There's also a time to say "Wait."
- Trust. Trust that God will stretch your time, fill in the gaps when you say no to responsibilities, and provide all of your needs according to his glorious riches (Philippians 4:19).
- Communicate with your spouse. Avoid trying to meet everyone's needs by yourself. Parenting is a partnership, so keep communication open with the other parent so you can tag-team responsibilities or meet your children's needs together. Good communication also involves accountability regarding busyness and priorities so that neither one of you misses what's most important during this season.
- Say no to unnecessary busyness so you can say yes to what's currently needed.
- Asses your social media use. How many minutes or hours a day is spent on social media rather than investing in people, self-care, or time with God?
- Avoid the entrapment of enabling. Are you busy doing things your kids should be doing for themselves? Remember, you're not a maid. You're a life giver. Is your young adult or teen needy to the extreme? Don't enable unhealthy behavior.
- Balance needs and self-care. Busyness that's driven by unbalanced priorities, insecurities, fear, or false guilt is an exhausting way to live. Are you chasing things that deplete you? Are you trying to fix your weaknesses instead of living in your strengths?
- Set appropriate boundaries for yourself, your kids, and others. A child of any age should not *demand* your time. Set boundaries that balance the needs of individual kids, your family, and you too. Implement the principles about

boundaries, enabling, entitlement, enmeshment, self-care, and grace in balance with what's healthy and appropriate for your situation.

- Communicate with your kids. Those family ties are important. Your kids at the releasing stage are old enough to understand when you have to prioritize one sibling over another or when you have a responsibility that conflicts with theirs. Remember that relationship parenting and fairness go a long way. Your children ultimately want to know that you see them and that you have their back.

- Don't be afraid to invest in *now.*

ETERNAL PRIORITIES | Pastor and Bible teacher Chuck Swindoll often teaches that only two things are eternal—God's Word and people. If I could share one principle for the releasing years, it would be this: Live intentionally for God's eternal kingdom and for the people most important to you. In that, you fulfill God's design of loving him and others and bringing glory and honor to him.

Living with an eternal perspective in your daily life shapes your time and priorities. If God is calling you to wait on a certain decision, promotion, project, or commitment because the timing isn't right, you can trust God for the results. On the other hand, if he is calling you to use your gifts during this season and it balances with your family, then trust God will provide for your family schedule.

I've learned there's no guilt when you're in the place you're supposed to be. Others may not understand it, but there's safety, security, and freedom when you obey Christ.

Life is not a race when God is in control. If you need to say no to something, he'll bring opportunities around again in his timing. He'll open and close doors at just the right time when you seek him and are obedient to the call.

GOING TOO FAST | When Mark, Drew, and Jenna left for college and the mission field, Ron and I considered opening our home for respite and hospitality through an online agency. It's something I've wanted to do since early in our marriage and was excited that our opportunity was on the horizon. We had three extra bedrooms now. Instead of waiting until Ethan left for college to make the rooms available, I thought we could do a trial run to learn the ropes.

We painted, we tiled the bathroom backsplash, and I collected lots of decorating ideas. The hands on work distracted me from my emotions over our emptier house.

Then disaster struck.

A water pipe broke when doing renovations in our upstairs bathroom. Water gushed from the second story all the way to the basement in a matter of minutes. There was significant water damage to the ceiling and floor, resulting in two weeks of running industrial-sized fans, doing reconstruction, installing drywall and carpet, and painting.

It was a mess.

At the same time, my father-in-law's health was rapidly declining. I had a busy speaking schedule, and we were spending all our time between our messy house, Ethan's sporting events, and the hospital. Ethan was home by himself a lot. I had clients in crisis and tragedy struck a good friend simultaneously.

Within two weeks, Ron's dad passed away.

Life dealt us things we hadn't anticipated. By the time our house was put back together, I was mentally, emotionally, and physical exhausted.

Life—midlife especially—contains big interruptions you can't plan. Through the stress of the unexpected house repairs, illness, and death, I learned that my threshold for crisis was different than it was years ago. It's exhausting to take care of parents and kids and still have energy for work and other responsibilities.

Unnecessary busyness takes on a new perspective when you truly want to be with those most important to you. Your kids. Your parents. Your closest friends and extended family. These are people with whom you aren't guaranteed time unless you make it a priority now.

Some things you grab hold of, and some things you let go. There's only *now* to hold on to what's most important.

BUILDING UP
and letting go

Father, thank you for the obstacles you put in my life to remind me of what's important. Help me to not be too busy with unnecessary things and miss time with those I love. Thank you for giving me discernment and wisdom, and thank you that I can trust your plan. Amen.

1. What activities or priorities currently pull you away from those most important to you?

2. What practical tips can you implement right now to shape better priorities?

3. What did you find most challenging in this chapter?

4. What did you find most encouraging in this chapter?

22

Mama's Growing Up

Well done, good and faithful servant!
—MATTHEW 25:23

Jenna walked away from the curb, pulling two heavy suitcases. Rain beat down on the car as I watched her walk toward the airport entrance. As she turned away from the car, I took a snapshot, because the moment was a big one, and I wanted to make sure I recorded it.

Mama had no tears.

Though I'd dropped her off for an international flight many times before, it was the first time I didn't tear up after saying goodbye. At the beginning of her other previous trips, tears came as I worried about her travel. If she'd arrive okay. If she'd return safely home.

Now in her midtwenties, Jenna is a seasoned traveler, doing orphan care between the United States and Latin America. She's growing up. And so am I.

My friend Carrie emailed me recently with a similar scene. Her son took a job several states away. He was one of those boomerang kids who moved back home because of a crisis. He's back on track now, and he is doing what he loves. I have her permission to share what she said: "I haven't shed one tear of sadness over him leaving. I feel sad he'll be farther away. I'm sad because I didn't get to hug him goodbye and I don't know when I'll see him again. But when you see the hand of God at work in your child's life, there are only tears of joy to be shed!"

Amen to that. There's a moment in this parenting mess when joy comes from seeing your kids at good places. When you've fought the good fight, run the race well, and have kept the faith (2 Timothy 4:7). When you witness the hand of the living God in the lives of your children and in your own life. When you walk away from your kids and want to say, "Look kids—no tears!"

From the first day of kindergarten to the moment of No Tears, you're a warrior in battle, an athlete running a race, and a big girl with childlike faith.

Because as your kids grow up, you do too.

THE CHANGING SEASONS | No one knows the journey you'll walk with your family between now and when you let that last child go. No one, that is, except God. He sees the tears, heartache, and pain you think will crush you. He knows the mountains you'll climb and the valleys you'll walk with each of your kids. But as you round the last corner to the finish line, Jesus says, "Well done, good and faithful servant" (Matthew 25:23).

As you celebrate each child's victorious milestones, you're celebrating, too. You've grown and developed stronger wing feathers with each child, though you may not feel like it. Now it's your time to soar as your kids spread their wings. It's time to weep and laugh and mourn and dance. As Ecclesiastes 3:1-8 says,

> There is a time for everything, and a season for every activity
>   under the heavens:
>   a time to be born and a time to die,
>   a time to plant and a time to uproot,
>   a time to kill and a time to heal,
>   a time to tear down and a time to build,
>   a time to weep and a time to laugh,
>   a time to mourn and a time to dance,

a time to scatter stones and a time to gather them,
a time to embrace and a time to refrain from embracing,
a time to search and a time to give up,
a time to keep and a time to throw away,
a time to tear and a time to mend,
a time to be silent and a time to speak,
a time to love and a time to hate,
a time for war and a time for peace.

There *is* a time to scatter the stones and to fledge those arrows. And there will be a time when they gather again.

Psalm 30:5 says, "Weeping may stay for the night, but rejoicing comes in the morning." No matter what hardships or grief you'll experience during this season, there is joy and contentment right along with it. Like Carrie, I've had tears of joy seeing each of my children mature, overcome obstacles, and excel in their giftings. There's immense gratification seeing your kids grow into the people God's created them to be. There's also happiness seeing a new, personal horizon around the corner once you get used to the idea. And those anticipated grandkids? The idea is growing on me each year I get closer to the empty nest.

Growing with our kids is an example of God's natural grace embedded in the cycle of life. Seasons come and they go. You've been in the days of summer for a long, beautiful period. But autumn is coming. The leaves are starting to fall. Before you know it, your colors will change to be the vibrant and beautiful reflection of God's plan for you in the next stage of your life.

There's a time to grow, and with growth comes change.

And though your parenting season changes, you never stop being a parent. Growing pains and parent insecurities don't go away. There are still challenges parenting adult children and grandchildren; new obstacles, new heartaches, new uncertainties. Though filled with pride when Mark graduated from his university, as his wedding neared, I wondered if we raised him to be a good husband. Just when you think you've got the parenting thing mastered, you wonder if you got it right.

We parents aren't perfect. There are lessons and new perspectives to learn from every parenting experience. When you allow your kids to struggle, you learn they can survive adversity. With each child who leaves the nest, you see the bigger picture of life after high school. When your young adults thrive and find their rhythm, you have assurance your younger kids will make it through their current struggles, too.

Jeremiah 29:11 says God has plans for a hope and a future—not only for our kids, but also for you and I. God's growing us as much as he's growing them. We're still stretched. We still feel uncertain. But the more accepting we are of *where* we are, it's easier to receive his grace.

APPROACHING THE FINISH LINE | When I ran the thirteen mile half marathon, I felt great at the start. My energy was high, the music was pumping, and the sun was shining. I felt like I could accomplish anything. By mile 5, monotony set in and my energy waned. My pace slowed and the remaining eight miles seemed daunting. By mile eight, I was getting discouraged. Though I was half way done, my knees started to hurt. The pain worsened over the next three miles and I thought the race would never end. The only motivation to continue was my refusal to be picked up by the bus that carried the slowest stragglers of the race. By mile 10, I wanted to quit. I had no desire to finish. I was tired, my body hurt, and there was no one around me to cheer me on. Then, at mile eleven, my energy increased because I knew the end was near. I thought about Ron waiting for me at the finish line, so I persevered through the pain and discouragement. When I turned the corner and saw my destination, with the loud music and festivities, I was glad I pushed through the pain for the joy and celebration on the other side.

Childrearing is similar. When your energy and hope wanes, there's confidence and encouragement knowing Jesus is on the other side of the finish line, already sharing in your victory. Psalm 23 gives beautiful imagery of Jesus with us on the parenting journey. He walks with you in the valley of the shadow of death, and you know he will do so again and again. You feel the comfort of his protective rod and staff on dark, lonely days. When you battle the spiritual enemy for you and your family, God abundantly provides for you and anoints you as his own. And in the years to come, goodness and mercy will follow you all the days of your life.

God is with you during these last few years of raising kids. He is cheering you on through discouragement and is waiting to celebrate with you.

Whether you feel like it or not, you're a champion. Your experiences, for better or for worse, have shaped and strengthened you. Some of your wounds have made you wiser; others have made you more confident. Though you may feel old, worn out, or out of your mind, with each step you've taken, freedom grows to be right where you are.

BEING THE LOCKER ROOM LOSER | It's a tradition in our small, rural high school for sports moms to decorate their team's locker rooms at the end of the regular season, before the state competitions begin. I've been decorating locker rooms for over a decade, and it always comes at a busy time. When it was time to decorate Ethan's cross-country locker room his sophomore year, it was during the disaster week of our water damage, and Ron's dad was in and out of the hospital. Decorating was the last thing I wanted to do.

As in years past, I grabbed the bag of decorating supplies I kept in a closet—but what was there was left over from Drew's senior basketball season the past spring. It was a measly collection of crepe paper, markers, colored masking tape, and a few glittery stars. I didn't have time to get more, so I brought what I had, anticipating other moms would have better decorations than I did.

They did. I showed up and met enthusiastic moms with an arsenal of newly purchased decorating supplies. For several of the moms, it was their first time decorating a locker room, so they looked to me and a couple of other moms for instructions and how-tos. They were excited to make the locker room look the best for their kids. Standing there, unprepared and unenthusiastic with my sorry stash of decorating supplies, I felt like the oldest, most pathetic loser mom there was.

Even in the best of your seasoned mom moments, you're still human. I struggled with guilt and shame over not being fully invested in the comradery. I felt out of place among the younger, more energetic women who were excited about cheering their kids on to the next level. My mind and heart were absent. I had a client in crisis, and I was waiting for Ron's call because he had taken his dad to the emergency room, again. Though I didn't know it at the time, within ten days, my father-in-law would pass away.

I deferred to the other seasoned moms to lead the festivities that night. Taking my pathetic bag of loser-mom supplies, I went to the urinals and taped streamers around a sign I made that said "Aim for the Stars." It was a decorating trick I learned from seasoned locker room moms who had mentored me.

Those Pinterest chicks couldn't top that.

I stood there, taping things to cement walls, and had those weird feelings again. Those biggest-moments-of-life feelings. I wanted to cry because there were only a few more times I'd be in a high school locker room with tape and streamers. I thought about all the women I'd decorated with, the different teams my kids had played on, and how excited I was at other times to cheer my kids on in their tourneys. I thought about my first time mom insecurities making team meals for Jenna's volleyball team, and how glad I was that my days of cooking for thirty team members were almost done.

I thought about the friendships I missed and how disconnected I felt among my peers in the moment. I fought back tears. I couldn't blame the younger moms for the enthusiasm they had. They didn't know my father-in-law was dying and I hadn't seen Ethan in days because we were with Grandpa each night. They didn't know my daughter had just called from Mexico, crying about her grandpa's decline, and that I really didn't care how many more posters were needed on the bulletin boards. They didn't know I had to call the college boys and prepare them about Grandpa's health, and that Ethan needed me at home rather than in his locker room that evening.

I told the moms I needed to leave early after the urinal master-piece and a few other posters were finished. While I shared with them about my father-in-law being in the hospital, I couldn't put words to the big case of mom grief going on inside: the grief you have as a midlife parent whose kids are leaving, whose parents are dying, and whose life is changing faster than you can imagine.

GROWING IN MOM GRACE | When I think of the mom I want to be after my kids fledge, I think of Evelyn, a woman I met when speaking at a women's event. I stayed overnight in her home and was blessed by her hospitality. Her husband had died a few years before and we sat up late talking about their life together. She talked with fondness about each of her four adult children and their families. As I listened to her, I was impacted by her experiences as a mother.

Her oldest son and his family were missionaries and she hadn't seen them for several years. Another son, a former prodigal child, was now a pastor and he and his wife were passionate about adoption because of their own infertility. Her youngest child had just married in her midthirties after being single. Evelyn's other daughter had recently become a widow: her husband had died just a few months before, leaving her alone with four school age children. Evelyn showed me the most recent family picture with all her kids, which had been taken five years earlier. She shared the names of each child and grandchild, noting that each of them were currently walking with God.

As I listened to Evelyn, I wondered what experiences my kids would have over the next twenty or more years. My heart grieved with hers as I realized the hard things her kids experienced, espe-cially her daughter's recent tragedy. I identified with her as a mom of a missionary and the caveats which accompany that experience.

What impacted me about Evelyn was the peaceful security that radiated from her. She didn't lament over her daughter being a new single mom, or about her other children's struggle with loneliness, infertility, or walking away from the faith for a season. She didn't fuss over her son living far away and rarely seeing his family, or the fact that several years had passed since her children were all together.

Instead, she exuded the simple elegance of mom grace. These struggles, losses, and grief did not define her, her family, or her God.

Evelyn gave me a gift that night, one I cling to when I miss all my kids being home or worry about their future. Her peaceful security didn't result from her children having pain free journeys. It came from the heritage she and her husband established on Christ's firm foundation. *He* built their family. The winds blew, the storms came, and their house and heritage stood firm.

I remember Evelyn when I feel like I'm falling apart, when I battle letting go, and when I fear growing older. Her journey gives me hope when I'm anxious about hardships my family may face or when I wonder when my family will all be together. She is the example of the woman I want to be in seasons to come; one whose house is built on the Lord, and whose children ultimately walk with God.

Between now and when we're an Evelyn, we must "let go and let God," taking our hands off our children so *he* can build a Christ-like heritage.

Our hands aren't empty after letting go: they're open. It's from this posture we receive the riches of God's grace he's ready to pour out.

Will you join me in opening your hands and heart as we release our children? Will you enter the comfort of his grace as we trust him for their future? As Hebrews 11:1 says, may we be sure of what we hope for and certain of what we cannot see.

Stand tall, warrior, and embrace God's grace. You've fought the good fight. You've finished the race. You've kept the faith.

Receive your reward: *Well done, my good and faithful servant.*

BUILDING UP
and letting go

Jesus, thank you for being with me every step of the way in my parenting journey. Thank you for knowing the grief, emotions, and highs and lows of experiences I've walked through alone. Thank you for each of my children and their journeys. Thank you for the joy you've given us and the pain you've seen us through. As I walk through the fledging journeys yet to come, help me to have faith in what you are already doing. Equip me with strength for what is to come, trusting in your complete provision for all of my family's needs. Amen.

1. What words of encouragement do you need to hear as you reach the finish line of letting go?

2. List things for which you're thankful to God. How has God faithfully provided for your family?

3. What are your biggest takeaways as you finish this book?

Epilogue

Between the time I typed the first words of this manuscript and the time the book is released, our family has gone through and will undergo more changes. It's a testimony to the multiple transitions that happen within this season of life.

I could add a new story, caveat, or experience every month. Time does not slow down. Two children are truly fledged from our home, and we're getting used to just one kid in college and one in high school. Our youngest is adjusting to being the only child at home, and Ron and I are enjoying more moments when it's just the two of us.

There are fewer tears. I don't long for those little ones as much as I used to, and grandkids would be welcome any time. I'm not as nervous having a daughter live in another country. She's healthy and thriving, and that means a lot.

Yet other things are on the horizon. Two friends of ours recently died; one in her forties and one in her fifties. Other friends have cancer. Suddenly life is put in perspective. I'm challenged to truly live what and who is most important. Family. Friends. My Lord, Jesus Christ.

Life continues to present unpredictable events reminding me there are no guarantees in life. Nothing is certain—nothing, that is, except the sovereignty and grace of Jesus Christ, and the here and now. The moments we're now living are the only ones we have.

My hope and prayer as you fledge your children is that you'll live boldly and love deeply both within your family and in your sphere of influence. You won't be afraid to text someone to let them know you're thinking of them. You'll put off unnecessary busyness so you can be there for someone important to you. You'll risk doing something you'd never thought you'd do, rather than assuming you can do it another day. And you'll dive deep into your relationship with Jesus Christ.

My father-in-law prayed for you that evening he prayed blessing over Ron and I before he died: I received the offer for this book contract earlier that day. He prayed for each of you and your families, and for God to be glorified through these words.

That's my prayer too. I pray God's fullness will draw us as mothers, fathers, and influencers to live boldly for his glory within our families and communities so others will know Jesus in a disconnected and hopeless world. May we follow him with the same passion and excitement we have for our children, no matter our age or season of life.

Blessings to you. If this book has helped or encouraged you, or if you'd like for me to speak at an event on any of these topics, I'd love to hear from you at brenda@brendayoder.com.

Appendix

Families of Children with Special Needs

There's a special place in the heart of God for you as a caretaker of a child with special needs. A special need is defined by a physical, cognitive, mental, or emotional disability that requires a child or adult to receive support, guidance, or individual care. Your family has dynamics unlike others, and I want to encourage you as your home changes during these years.

Your mom grief may have different layers than those of other parents. Your childrearing journey may never quite be finished because of the needs of your child. Here are a few words of encouragement as you walk through your changing family and midlife:

- Take care of yourself. No matter where you are in your parenting journey, self-care is important. Find a few things that bring you joy and peace and work them into your routine or lifestyle. Speak up for your needs to your spouse and adult children. Though you may be the primary caregiver for your child, you are not the only one capable of providing care for short periods of time. Enlist a young adult child, a friend from church, an extended family member, or a neighbor to help in areas that give you time to breathe and recharge.

- Seek respite when needed. If your child or adult with special needs requires twenty-four-hour care, seek services in your area or support within your church so you can have a break or do things with your other kids.

- Consider yourself a *caregiver* rather than just a mom. There's a difference between the two roles. You are a mom to all your children, and you are a caregiver to your child with special needs. If you have other kids at home, they still need you as mom. Delegate certain caregiving tasks for your child with special needs to others so you can also engage with your other kids. Enlist a support team from church or agencies in the community that provide caregiving or respite services. Seek out caregiver support groups or services that specialize in caregiver needs.

- Allow your child or adult with special needs to be a part of the family but not the center of the family. This is difficult, because this child's needs probably absorb your time, energy, and resources. As much as you can, though, pull your other kids who are at home into the center of the family alongside their sibling. Cling to the family unit, not just one child.

- If your child has a mental health or behavioral disorder that is harmful or toxic to other family members, get support for the children still at home. Get them involved in sports or activities with their peers so that their lives are not defined by their sibling's needs or disabilities. If you have an adult child with mental health issues who is not taking care of herself or has stopped taking critical medication, draw boundaries as needed for the health and safety of minor kids. Beware of enabling an adult who is responsible and capable to take care of his own needs.

Each child, family, and situation is different. This is not an exhaustive list of how to be a caregiver for children or young adults with special needs. It's important to acknowledge the impact such a child or adult has on any minor children in the home. The needs of the minor children are important too. Don't try to be everything to everyone alone.

And in everything, give yourself grace. Let Christ carry you.

The Author

BRENDA L. YODER is a national speaker, author, Bible teacher, life coach, licensed mental health counselor, and parent of teens and young adults. She has a master's degree in clinical mental health counseling and a bachelor's degree in education. A former high school teacher and middle school counselor working with kids and parents across the socioeconomic spectrum, she and her family live in  Shipshewana, Indiana. Connect with her at brendayoder.com.